Politics and Protest

To: Ambassador Collins
Best of luck in D.C. - I hope
you enjoy "Experiencing America!"

Cheers.
Patrick Reilly

Patrick Reilly

Politics and Protest

How Political Systems Influenced the American and Northern Ireland Civil Rights Movement

VDM Verlag Dr. Müller

Imprint

Bibliographic information by the German National Library: The German National Library lists this publication at the German National Bibliography; detailed bibliographic information is available on the Internet at http://dnb.d-nb.de.

Cover image: www.purestockx.com

Publisher:
VDM Verlag Dr. Müller Aktiengesellschaft & Co. KG
Dudweiler Landstr. 125 a, 66123 Saarbrücken, Germany
Phone +49 681 9100-698, Fax +49 681 9100-988, Email: info@vdm-verlag.de

Produced in USA and UK by:
Lightning Source Inc., La Vergne, Tennessee, USA
Lightning Source UK Ltd., Milton Keynes, UK

ISBN: 978-3-8364-3856-8

Politics and Protest: How Political Systems Influenced the American and Northern
Ireland Civil Rights Movements

ABSTRACT

Social movements are not created in a vacuum. The nature of the political system in which social movements operate influences the strategies chosen by leaders. The question becomes why do some leaders chose to remain peaceful, working through the existing political structure and why do some choose to become violent? In systems that have an independent judiciary, numerous electable ideologies and a federal system of government leaders of social movements are encouraged to work through the system to accomplish their goals. In systems that do not have these characteristics, social movements must work outside the system, often times aiming to destroy the existing political system in the process. For them, achieving their goals is not possible in the current environment. This study is a closer examination of those dimensions of the hypothesis through a case study of the African-American Civil Rights movement in the United States and the Catholic Civil Rights movement in Northern Ireland.

DEDICATION

To John Henderson, without your enthusiasm, experience, and optimism this project would have never been finished. You always had the right mix of "kick in the butt" and kind words that I needed. To Eric Juenke, your guidance and suggestions are a large part of this work. To the women of the sorority system at the University of Colorado at Boulder, especially the Panhellenic Executive Board. Your energy, optimism, and "can-do" spirit got me through many long days. And most of all, to my parents, Kevin and Alice Reilly. You installed in me at an early age, the attitude that I can do anything I put my mind to. Your love and support over the past twenty-seven years has shown me how true that is.

Thank you to all of you from the bottom of my heart; you are all a part of this.

TABLE OF CONTENTS

FIGURES

Social movement theory provides a rich, complex view of how individuals in a society come together to agitate for change. A social movement is action composed of "collective challenges by people with common purposes and solidarity in sustained interactions with opponents and authorities (Tarrow 1994, 3)." These theories describe how individuals gather momentum, how organizations form, how they decide on directions, strategies and ideologies. Some theories emphasize culture, while some emphasize resources. The common thread that runs through all social movement theory is that they all attempt to explain group action.

Social scientists have classically looked at social movements as groups composed of "irrational" individuals (McAdam 1992, 1) in response to Mancur Olson's study of collective action. The field has shifted in recent years to focus on mass behavior, but still neglects the interactions between social movements and the political and cultural institutions they purport to change. Political scientists have not fared much better. Most of their discussion has looked exclusively at power through established institutional structures. Groups that operate outside the established channels, such as social movements, have been marginalized. The "political opportunity structures" model of social movements is an attempt to combine the most useful aspects of theories developed by sociologists and political scientists.

Resource mobilization theory is within the same vein as the "political opportunity structures" model. It attempts to explain the actions of social movements through the rational choices of their leaders. These leaders possess finite resources and therefore choose strategies aimed at best exploiting the limited opportunities they have (Schrager

1985, 858). To them, a social movement is a rational strategy of pursuing goals through collective action. Most of the research with regards to this model focuses on the internal dynamics of social movements, i.e. the recruitment structure, the internal decision making structure, the selection of strategy (Rose 1997, 461). Research mobilization theory tends to assume the institutional nature of constraints that social movements face. The "political opportunity structures" model as introduced by Kitschlet (1986) uses these constraints to explain the strategies chosen by social movements.

The classic model of social movements attempts to explain the process through "strains and deprivations" in society (Pinard 1969, 358). The "strain" on society then has a disruptive effect and leads to an aggregate threshold of "equally disturbed states of mind." This threshold is necessary for the mobilization of a social movement (see figure 1, McAdam 1992, 7).

Structural Strain ⟶ Disruptive psychological state ⟶ Social Movement
Figure 1

The existence of strains and relative deprivation is however, "a necessary, but not sufficient condition of social protest" (Kerbo 1982, 648). The classical model possesses an insensitivity to the variations present in social movements. Differences in opportunity are not random occurrences, they are structurally shaped. Many scholars, including Kitschelt (1986) and Kerbo (1982), have noted that "strains and deprivations" do not in and of themselves explain differences in the courses of action chosen by social movement elites.

Social movements are not created in a vacuum. The environment in which they exist influences everything from the way they're formed, to strategies undertaken, to what is considered a success. The leaders of these groups make choices about the developmental path their movements will take. These decisions are based on the rational calculation of which strategies are most likely to lead to success. Social movements are not monolithic. Within the movement there are different groups competing for attention, resources and members. Leaders pick strategies that will make their group the most successful, however success is defined. They are entrepreneurs trying to maximize their return (Bianco 1990, 137). If leaders feel they can work through the existing political structure then they will pursue a strategy of conciliation and assimilation. If the existing system does not provide a way for them to maintain their leadership or keep the group going, leaders may adopt a strategy of working outside the system and try to structurally reform, or destroy, the system itself.

This work starts with an examination of the role of leadership in solving the collective action problem. I then introduce my hypothesis, that an independent judiciary, numerous electable ideologies, and a federal system of government create conditions which encourage leaders of social movements to pursue strategies of assimilation. An examination of the "political opportunity structure" model follows. I then introduce my case studies, the African-American Civil Rights Movement in the United States and the Catholic Civil Rights Movement in Northern Ireland, and discuss why they were chosen. A brief history of each movement is given. I then look at the role that an independent judiciary plays in influencing social movement strategy and look at this role in both the United States and Northern Ireland. An examination of how the number of electable ideologies and a federal system of government influences the strategies of social movement leaders follows. Each of these explanations is applied to a case study of the African-American and Catholic Civil Rights Movements. The work ends with a conclusion about the strategy of social movement leaders in democracies and introduces further areas of study.

The Catholic and the African-American Civil Rights Movements were chosen because they were similar movements with similar goals. They took place at roughly the same time in history. Additionally, at the time the Civil Rights Movements were taking place, both the United States and Northern Ireland were democracies. That they chose different paths, violence in Northern Ireland and non-violent resistance in the U.S., despite both being democracies, cries out for explanation.

LEADERSHIP AND THE COLLECTIVE ACTION PROBLEM

Leaders of social movements are either the most morally committed members of the group or risk-taking entrepreneurs who will profit from the success of the movement (Chong 1991, 140). Political entrepreneurs are those individuals who are willing to "pay the costs of soliciting and coordinating contributions in exchange for individual benefits such as power, prestige, or a share of the profits (Chong 1991, 122)." A leadership position in a social movement requires not only the willingness to take risks, but also the credentials and social standing to make the risk-taking viable. Potential activists will sit out and assess the prospect of success for collective action. They will only decide to join when they feel that enough other people will join the movement to make it viable. The problem for organizing social movements is when too many people think this. Everyone is waiting for everyone else to join up (Heckathorn 1996, 259). In this situation it is the leader's job to help the group overcome this hesitation or tipping point. There is a heavy start-up cost to be paid by leaders to transform the collective action dilemma into an "assurance game[1] (Oliver 1985, 535)."

The problem of organizing public-spirited collective action requires overcoming the "free-rider problem" or the prisoner's dilemma. With regards to the civil rights movement in both the United States and Northern Ireland, how do you convince people to get beat-up? One way is to think about collective action as an "assurance game." In the "assurance game" model, it is in the interest of participants to work together (unlike

---

[1] In the assurance game if "everyone else cooperates, then one has an incentive to cooperate as well." While in the prisoner's dilemma, individuals are better off defecting when everyone else cooperates. The incentives that exist in the prisoner's dilemma encourage participants to double-cross each other. In the assurance game the best case scenario for any individual can only be achieved when everyone cooperates. The difference between the two games is that it is tough to achieve mutual cooperation in the prisoner's dilemma; while in the assurance game communication and coordination can assure mutual cooperation (Chong 1991, 104).

in the "prisoner's dilemma" model), however this is only the case if the participants can be assured that they "share a common understanding of their predicament (Chong 1991, 104)." To get to this common understanding and overcome the "free-rider problem" of collective action two conditions must exist:

1. Success must be likely.

2. There must be enough people $(v-1)^2$ to succeed.

When the prospect of achieving the goals of the social movement is low, the threshold (v-1) for people to participate is high (Heckathorn 1996, 259). There are certain strategies that leaders of social movements can pursue to create these conditions. The first is to lower the barrier to entry. This can occur by making participation in collective action as easy as possible and facilitating communication between individuals so that they may be sure that others will also participate (Kollock 1998, 194). Additionally leaders can increase the selective benefits of participating. They can increase the social pressure on bystanders to participant. And finally, leaders can make sure the prospect and path to success are clear. In the case of the civil rights movement these strategies were accomplished by organizing collective action through existing groups (Oliver 1985, 542), mostly churches and religious groups in both Northern Ireland and the United States. Communication was easier, the knowledge that others would actually participate was more secure, and the costs to reputation for those not willing to participate were higher.

The more credible a leader is, "we will achieve our goal by taking action x," and then that goal is achieved by taking action x, the more effective the leader is in persuading potential members to join. This makes the selection of a successful strategy extremely important. If leaders are preaching a strategy that does not produce results, the

---

[2] v is the number of people necessary for collective action to succeed.

leader will soon go out of business. On the other hand, publicity about early successes will attract more members (Taylor 1986, 161). More members will join, in turn meaning that the threshold for joining (v-1) will be reached for more people considering joining the social movement. Another way leaders can attract participants to their social movement is by lowering the cost to entrance (Knoke 1988, 313). Due to the potential costs (to both life and property) associated with a violent strategy, non-violent social movements have an easier time overcoming the tipping point associated with the "assurance game" and "free-rider" dilemma "because of the lower risk (Chong 1991, 32)." In the United States leaders of the Civil Rights Movement such as Martin Luther King, Jr. and Thurgood Marshall of the NAACP had already gained a foothold within the existing political system through the courts with *Brown v. Board of* Education and with the electorate through northern whites. They had achieved these gains in an open system because of judicial review (court ordered desegregation), a dominant national government (the integration of Little Rock High and the integration of the Army), and by electing government officials friendly to their cause (the 1960 presidential election). These initial gains made it essential that the leaders were able to maintain the non-violent nature of their movements if they did not want to lose their hard-won allies. If a violent strategy had won out, the leaders who had previously advocated a non-violent strategy would have suffered massive reputational and power costs (Chong 1991, 48). These leaders had an intense interest in maintaining a non-violent strategy so that they could preserve their positions as leaders.

Mancur Olson has argued that the moral and reputational incentives offered to activists have no bearing on their participation in social movements, "it is not possible to definitely say whether or not a given individual acted for moral reasons or for other reasons in some particular case (Oslon 1971, 61)." Individuals must be motivated/enticed by private selective incentives in order to participate in social movements or else they "free-ride" (Olson 1971, 51). This explanation is faulty however because it assumes that the rational individual participating in collective action is only interested in his own personal interests (Olson 1971, 7). This confuses economic and political behavior. In the economic marketplace individuals will cooperate with whoever will give them the highest possible return (Chong 1991, 33). Participants in social movements however will not indiscriminately support whatever moment will benefit them the most personally. Most likely one condition of joining a social movement is the fact that one's personal goals are aligned with the goals of the movement he or she is joining. The calculations made by individuals for economic and political concerns are different, "whether [or not] one's taste for chocolate affects one's propensity to take a job in a chocolate factory, surely one's taste for civil rights affects one's propensity to join in a civil rights movement (Fireman 1979, 14)." In order to pass the tipping point in the "assurance game," leaders must convince individuals that the goals and strategies of the social movement are similar to their individual goals.

The more success a social movement has, the more it raises the reputational costs for not being a part of the movement. This will encourage other leaders to participate who are worried about saving face (Knoke 1988, 313). Charismatic leaders are helpful to this endeavor, not because they are charismatic however. They are helpful because they can easier/better convince potential members of the prospect for success (Chong 1991, 122).

Leaders are essential to any social movement because they bear the majority of the initial costs of overcoming the "free-rider" problem. They provide leadership when costs of participation are high and constitute a "critical mass" within the social movement. Such individuals, people willing to risk the most and support the movement when its success is least likely, are rare but necessary for social movement success. Their rarity may explain why social movements are so often unsuccessful. The existence of relatively few of these individuals, the leaders of movements, makes choosing the correct strategies that much more significant in convincing others that the potential for success exists and then spurring them to join.

Social movements exist in the context of the political system that encompasses them. The strategies chosen by the leaders of the groups are picked in response to numerous factors, including the nature of the political system of the country in which the social movement is forming. In states with an independent judiciary, numerous electable ideologies, and a federalist system the leaders of social movements will be more likely to choose strategies that attempt to work within the existing political system. If a social movement forms in a state without an independent judiciary, only one electable ideology, and political power concentrated in the hands of a few, the leaders of social movements are more likely to choose strategies that work outside the existing political structure. This type of political system encourages leaders to pursue a strategy of confrontation.

The African-American Civil Rights Movement in the United States was taking place in a political system where the courts had the power of judicial review, a supreme national government could overrule discriminatory decisions of state and local governments, and candidates favorable to their cause could be elected to public office. Because of these characteristics, the leaders of the most popular and successful social movements pursued strategies of assimilation and worked through the existing system to achieve their goals. The Catholic Civil Rights movement in Northern Ireland was taking place in a political system where the courts did not have the power of judicial review, the national government based in London was not supreme in most policy areas, and candidates favorable to their cause could not win elections. Due to these characteristics, the leaders of the most popular and successful social movements pursued strategies of confrontation to achieve their goals and used violence to try to destroy the existing

political system.

Political Opportunity Structure

Not all social movements are created in the same environment. Differences in the availability of resources, historical records and institutional arrangements create situations which influence the actions and choices of their leaders. Sometimes these characteristics constrain action and sometimes they incite action. Harold Kitschelt defined these characteristics in his 1986 study of the anti-nuclear movement as "political opportunity structures" (Kitschelt 1986, 62). "Political opportunity structure" can be defined in numerous ways. However, the general consensus within the discipline has consolidated around the four dimensions defined by Douglas McAdams, a key scholar of the movement (McAdam 1996, 26):

1. The closed or open nature of the institutional political system.
2. The stability or lack thereof in the elite coalitions which typically run the political system.
3. The presence or absence of social movement allies amongst the governing elites.
4. The state's ability and inclination for repression.

The risks associated with collective action by social movements are not completely politically determined, however. Historical experiences and cultural myths may produce different results from the same action. "Political opportunity structures" force leaders of social movements to choose from options available to them that are likely to result in success (Koopmans 1999, 97). Charles Tilly (1978), Sidney Tarrow (1994), and McAdams (1996) all wrote about how the choices available to leaders of social movements are influenced by the motivations, resources and capacity of the social movements. Opportunity alone cannot explain the resultant strategy.

Social movement scholars distinguish between two different types of political opportunity structures, closed and open. The dominance of one type of system or the other sets the parameters for behavior of the leaders of social movements. In his study of American protest behavior, Peter Eisinger identified a linear relationship between the nature of a political system and the strategies chosen by leaders of social movements. The more open a system, the more likely the leaders will pursue assimilation; the more closed a regime, the more likely leaders will choose to confront the regime (see figure 2, Eisinger 1973, 12).

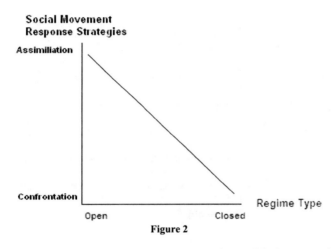

Figure 2

Four factors determine the composition of the political system in a country (Goodwin 1999, 32). First, the larger the number of parties, the tougher it is for a "ruling cartel" to limit the participation of groups that are outside the established bureaucratic system, such as social movements. Second, the more independent and powerful the legislature is, the more open the system is. If the legislature can control policy outcomes independent of the executive branch, it makes it easier for groups who can mobilize voters, such as social movements, to have a measurable effect on policy. Third, the more avenues of interaction that exist between the executive branch and those outside government, the more open the system is. Numerous access points exist for influencing

13

policy in a government where bureaucrats on different levels can make policy decisions independent of the elite. And finally, an independent judiciary is extremely important to the openness of the system. As Kitcshelt noted, it allows aggrieved minorities who cannot seek redress through elections another avenue to see that their complaints/demands are met (Kitschelt 1986, 63).

The measure of the openness of political systems is not a discrete measure, it is continuous. The different dimensions in which each of these measurements can be made mean there will be many different degrees of openness.

Certain institutions are characteristic of an open system. A large legislature in which many parties are represented is a common characteristic. The competition created by the numerous parties is essential in a polyarchy according to Robert Dahl (Dahl 1971, 2). A sprawling executive branch in which a large number of bureaucracies operate independently of each other is another. A judiciary that exercises its authority to police the other branches of government usually signals the necessary independence. A federal system in which multiple levels of government have discretion over policy is indicative of the numerous access points available in an open system. These institutions possess characteristics which encourage leaders to integrate their social movements into the political system.

By their very nature, political systems that are open support and reward strategies of assimilation. Social movements are encouraged to work through established political institutions and channels. Leaders can mobilize collective action within institutional bounds and still challenge opponents (Tarrow 1988, 427). Government officials in open systems are more receptive to including social movements into the policy-making process because inclusion benefits the members of the policy elite who can co-opt the social movement's goals and therefore, strengthen their own positions. Elites within the current system can increase their power and position in this manner. Protests and consternation promote a search for new policies in an open system to mollify these demands. An open system encourages leaders to pursue collective action through established channels as the most effective way to achieve change.

In an open system, social movements can influence, both directly and indirectly, the legislature. Elections provide an opportunity to place individuals with sympathetic views in positions of influence. The lobbying of key actors in both the executive and legislative branches gives social movements an opportunity to affect the implementation of policy. Social movements that possess large amounts of resources (both financial and manpower), can work through established party structures and influence the policy of legislatures who disagree with them (Schneider 1992, 737). An independent judiciary allows social movements with minority views to receive an audience for their complaints without having to convince the electorate of their position. Open systems also allow social movements to place issue referenda on ballots to give voters an opportunity to change policy directly (Nelkin 1978, 275).

Social movements in open systems are encouraged to work through, rather than against, the established system in order to achieve change. However, the structures present in other types of political systems may not encourage leaders to pursue this type of relationship. Some systems encourage confrontation as the most effective way of achieving goals.

A closed political system is one in which the judiciary branch is highly dependent on the executive branch for power. The executive branch is the most powerful branch of government, dominating a weak legislature. As Robert Gamer noted, "the highest power usually rests with a Prime Minister (or President)…whose policy decisions are seldom challenged by courts or legislatures (Gamer 1976, 165)." This leads to one branch being accountable for policy outcomes and reduces the ability of social movements to challenge policy because very few access points exist. The fewer the number of parties that can win elections, the more closed the system. A limited party system often has difficulty incorporating demands from movements that are not already a part of the established political structure (Decalo 1992, 9).

There are certain characteristics of closed systems which encourage the repression of social movements. The more control the existing regime has, the more limited the resources are to challenge existing policies. Those out of power tend to stay that way. A dependent judiciary creates a system in which courts are avenues for political arbitration. They exist as another instrument for the executive branch to suppress conflicting views (Kitschelt 1986, 64). Because government officials are primarily concerned with maintaining their own power, closed systems are also unable to react to the demands of new participants in the policy process (Decalo 1992, 8). The state views existing actors as the only individuals with legitimate policy demands and as such, actors challenging the status quo are prevented from working through existing policy channels. Unlike in open systems, policy-making is the prerogative of existing elites who do not need the consent of outsiders to govern and can simply close them out of the process. The insulated nature of the elites leads to limited reform. There is no need to co-opt social movement ideas when you have the ability to simply dismiss them. Closed systems respond to protest by maintaining their predetermined course.

Closed political systems possess considerable capacity for warding off the demands of social movements when they threaten existing policies. As a result, leaders of social movements adopt confrontational strategies. When no avenues exist within established structures to change or challenge policy, leaders will then direct their energy against the system rather than through it. Their goal is to be disruptive and work outside the established political channels. The more unwilling a regime is to address grievances, the greater the risk that this inflexibility will lead to demands beyond the pressing policy issues to the issue of regime legitimacy itself (Kitschelt 1986, 82). The inability of social movements to seek redress through existing structures will lead them to pursue a strategy of structural reform. The cumulative effect of all these actions is to create strong structural pressures. The existing regime must eliminate these structural pressures since they do not possess the institutions to accommodate them.

In closed systems, social movements lack the ability to initiate change through the political process. One of the few ways available to them to practice politics is through the use of violence. While this strategy may be costly, in a closed system the only other option available to leaders is to choose to do nothing. They make the calculation that doing nothing is more costly than pursuing violent political policies. A closed political system leads those outside the system, such as social movements, to confront and fundamentally alter the political system, often through violent means. Since the existing elite controls all the levers of influence, leaders of social movements outside the system have no other option but to try and alter the system itself.

Different types of political systems lead to the different strategies chosen by leaders of social movements. The "political opportunity structures" force them to choose from options available that are likely to result in success (Koopmans 1999, 97). It sets the menu of options for the leaders of social movements. However, the large number of interacting variables and the complex nature of the political world prevent the "political opportunity structure" model from explaining the difference in strategies chosen by leaders in its entirety.

A comparison of social movements with the same goals but different strategies lends itself to a cross-national study. The African-American Civil Rights movement in the United States and the Catholic Civil Rights movement in Northern Ireland is one such comparison. Leaders of the Civil Rights movement in Northern Ireland have noted that they originally attempted to model their movement after Martin Luther King, Jr.'s and Gandhi's strategies of non-violence (Power 1972, 223). Currently there exists a wealth of scholarly research on the American Civil Rights Movement, providing unparalleled descriptive detail. However, as case studies and not cross-national studies, this research does not provide the opportunity for a generalized understanding of the aspects that influence the dynamics of social movements or a cross-national comparison of theoretical conclusions.

A comparison of the Civil Rights Movements in Northern Ireland and the United States is an attempt at a systematic comparison of two strikingly similar social movements. In both places citizenship, "a status bestowed on those who are full members of the community," (Marshall 1950, 8) was limited to people who possessed certain characteristics: race in the United States and religion in Northern Ireland. The cases are well-suited to discovering the effects that "political opportunity structures" have on social movement leadership strategy for a number of reasons. Both movements started out with the goal of non-violent protests. Both movements were composed of minorities agitating for civil rights. Both were trying to overcome decades of repression. Both existed in political systems that had "first-past-the-post" electoral systems. They shared not only similar goals but similar opponents: entrenched majorities who occupied

19

positions of power in the existing government. These two places also existed within the democratic sphere of influence. The civil rights taken for granted by other citizens of the country had not been extended to everyone. Why did the Civil Rights Movement in the United States maintain its peaceful position while the one in Northern Ireland turned violent? This dichotomy makes their differences as important as their similarities. While it is useful to know how these social movements rose up and why they did it at that exact moment in history, that effort is beyond the scope of this work. This study is concerned with the strategies chosen by leaders once the social movements have already formed.

I am comparing racial cleavages in the United States with religious cleavages in Northern Ireland. The two cases are more similar than at first glance. Religion in Northern Ireland is unlike religion in the United States. The differences between Protestants and Catholics are not doctrinal. They are "not fighting over supernatural worship the essential element of any activity which defines itself as religious (Cairns 2000, 438)." The differences in religion encompass so much more. The words you use, the school you go to, the holidays you celebrate, the sports teams you support, the professions you can enter, even the names of towns are different for Catholics and Protestants[3]. The difference in religion is not a socially constructed issue. If you are born into a Catholic family you are Catholic forever, even if you are non-practicing and the same is true for Protestants (Rose 1976, 265). And while the differences in religion may not be as superficial as the differences in race (a black man is a black man no matter where he lives), they are just as "telling" to any citizen of Northern Ireland. The markers consist of "a person's name, area of residence, school attended, linguistic (and possibly

---

[3] One town in Northern Ireland is referred to as Londonderry by the Protestant government and Derry by it's mostly Catholics inhabitants (Elliot 1999, 229).

phonetic) usage, colour and symbolism of dress (Burton 1978, 37)." And while this may not be the most reliable indicator, its true importance is that citizens of Northern Ireland "have the desire and necessity to tell (Burton 1978, 38)." If you see your neighbor participating in "marching season" he is Protestant, if you do not he is Catholic (Cairns 2000, 441). The marches identify "who [the marchers] are, where they come from" for both themselves and others. There is no neutral sideline, and individuals are immediately identified with one of the groups. It does not matter if this is not the case; it is the perception and therefore reality. And while it may not be as visually apparent as race (although some claim that it is) everyone is placed into a group that they cannot change at birth. It is for this reason that the racial cleavages in the United States and religious cleavages in Northern Ireland provide adequate similarities for a comparison.

Is my argument spurious? What if the institutions do not create openness, but they merely reflect the openness already present in society? If this was the case, then the institutions that were created in Northern Ireland should be based on the historical conflict between Catholics and Protestants. Their creation merely institutionalized the feeling in society that Catholics should be second-class citizens. A closer examination however, shows that this is not the case. The government of Northern Ireland that was created as a result of the 1922 Anglo-Irish Treaty merely copied the existing governmental structure that already existed in the United Kingdom. A judicial system with no power of judicial review reflected centuries of English law tradition, where "questions of the validity of the enactments of the United Kingdom Parliament are not legal at all-they are political and historical (Narain 1975, 43)." The creation of a "first-past-the-post" electoral system was a reflection of the electoral system that existed in the

21

United Kingdom rather than religious tinkering with electoral politics (Duffy 1996, 125). The decision to make the only official control London had over Northern Ireland the ability to dissolve parliament was made jointly by the British and Irish governments (Graham 1994, 185).[4]   The institutions created in Northern Ireland did not simply reflect the nature of society at the time.

---

[4] The Irish pushed for this power sharing agreement because they felt that sooner rather than later the citizens of Northern Ireland would want to join the rest of Ireland. This belief is reflected in the 1937 Irish Constitution which enshrined in writing the idea that the Republic of Ireland consisted of the entire island (Graham 1994, 185).

On May 18, 1896, the United States Supreme Court issued its decision in the case of *Plessy v. Ferguson*. In this famous ruling, the Court upheld the idea of "separate, but equal (Groves 1951, 66)." As a result of the ruling there was an expansion of Jim Crow laws around the country. Whites and blacks were separated on street cars, taxi cabs and busses. "Colored" entrances appeared at all manner of businesses. Parks, drinking fountains, and even elevators where split into "white" and "colored" (Lyons 1998, 38).

The ruling had a stunning effect on the education situation for African-Americans. Ten years after the *Plessy* decision, schools in Georgia were spending "eighty cents for the white child and twenty on the Negro," according to the Georgia Equal Rights Convention. Twenty years after the ruling, the school system of South Carolina was spending "$12.37 on every white student, $1 for every Negro." There were only 64 high schools for African-American children in the entire South. Not one public medical or law school existed (Sterling 1968, 101). African-Americans had become second class citizens in their own country.

The system of segregation that had sprung up in the South soon spread around the country. Cities such as Chicago and New York concentrated their black population in ghettos with "gentleman's agreements." A gentleman's agreement was a contract signed by white property owners in which the "owner agrees not to exchange with, sell to, or lease to any member of a race not Caucasian." By 1930 over seventy-five percent of property owners in Chicago had signed such an agreement (Sterling 1968, 113). Those individuals who did manage to break through this barrier where treated horrendously in their new neighborhoods. At least 58 homes were bombed in Chicago, and two people were killed. Not one person was charged (Georges-Abeyie 1983, 306). The story was much of the same in Boston's Roxbury neighborhood, in Detroit's Paradise Valley. The South used Jim Crow laws to repress blacks; the North used "gentleman's agreements." Both had the same effect of perpetuating discrimination against African-Americans.

In response to this treatment, a burgeoning Civil Rights Movement amongst the African-American community began to emerge. Tired of living as less than full citizens, leaders began to agitate for full civil rights. As W.E.B. Du Bois declared, "We claim for ourselves every single right that belongs to a free born American, political, civil and social (Sterling 1968, 117)." In 1910 the National Association for the Advancement of Colored People (NAACP) was formed. This important group was formed to "promote the equality of rights and eradicate racial prejudice; to advance the interest of colored people; to secure for them impartial suffrage; and to increase their opportunities for securing justice in the courts, education for their children, employment according to their ability and complete equality before the law (NAACP Mission Statement 2006)." Working in conjunction with the National Urban League, the NAACP started programs to promote worker training, open health clinics and increase job openings. The programs were aimed at promoting "opportunity, not alms" for African-Americans (Eisenberg 1982, 112).

The Great Depression hit the African-American community hard. More than half of African-Americans of working age were unemployed. As such, the African-American Civil Rights Movement was one of the most ardent supporters of President Roosevelt and his "New Deal" programs (Hamilton 1992, 440). The "New Deal" programs combined with the industrial boom of World War II saw blacks leave the South en masse for factory

24

jobs in the North, a movement known as "The Great Migration (Morris 1999, 518)." As more and more blacks began showing up in the cities of the North, their electoral power increased. In 1928, Chicago sent its first black representative to Congress (Broussard 1984, 32). In 1944, New York followed suit, electing Adam Clayton Powell to the House of Representatives (Daniels 1973, 120). While the economic boom from World II and "the Great Migration" were creating new opportunities for many African-Americans, American society at-large still clung to a policy of segregation.

The NAACP was working through the court system to help ensure equal rights for African-Americans. Their strategy of using the legal system to seek civil rights gains saw results in 1938 with the Supreme Court's *Missouri v. Canada* ruling, which made the unconditional equality of blacks law (Agyeman 1991, 682). They won an additional victory in 1944 when the Court made all white primaries illegal in the *Smith v. Allwright* decision (Smith 1982, 40). Since the Democratic primary was essentially the election in the South, this gave African-Americans a chance to participate in electoral politics.

At the same time, groups were forming throughout the country to use mass resistance to pursue change. Several groups working together, including the NAACP, the National Urban League, and the National Council of Negro Women, organized a massive march on Washington D.C. scheduled for July 1, 1941. Hearing of the march, President Roosevelt asked two of the group's leaders, A. Philip Randolph and Walter White to the White House (Lewis 1991, 279). There they assured President Roosevelt that they did indeed have a march of "no less than 100,000 people" planned. In order to have the march called off President Roosevelt issued Executive Order 8802 on June 25, 1941, making discrimination in employment illegal (Collins 2001, 273).

Discrimination in education policy was once again rearing its ugly head in the South. The *Plessy* ruling had created separate schools, which were far from equal. Books, infrastructure, and teacher's pay were all neglected at schools which had majority African-American populations. Once again the NAACP stepped up and took the case to court (Russo 1994, 298). After 40 years of chipping away at "separate but equal," they decided to challenge the doctrine of segregation itself. And on May 17, 1954, the Supreme Court of the United States agreed, stating that "separate educational facilities are inherently unequal (Clark 1988, 126)." The Court ordered all schools in the country to desegregate.

The response throughout the South was one of resistance. Southern state legislatures passed almost 200 new segregation laws in the year after the ruling. While they might have been technically allowed to attend white schools, most black children were prevented through a combination of force and intimidation. With Southern states employing all manner of delaying tactics, in 1955, the Supreme Court issued the *Brown II* ruling. This ruling ordered the desegregation of public school systems in the United States to proceed with "all deliberate speed (Brookover 1993, 163)." While it took U.S. Army paratroopers in Little Rock, Arkansas, and U.S. Marshall's in Oxford, Mississippi, African-Americans had managed to integrate schools in the heart of the Deep South.

The 1950s saw the rise of the non-violent protest movement as part of the African-American Civil Rights movement. Led by the Martin Luther King, Jr., a program of mass non-violent protest started. Drawing on the ideas of Henry David Thoreau and Mahatma Gandhi, King asked that his followers not return violence with violence, "we must love our white brothers no matter what they do to us (Sterling 1968,

186).'' In 1955, his ideas were put to the test during Montgomery Bus Boycott. Protesting the arrest of a young black woman, Rosa Parks, for sitting in a seat reserved for white customers, King led a boycott of all segregated transportation services in Montgomery, Alabama. After a year of falling revenue, the bus companies of Mobile finally relented and allowed any paying customer to sit in any seat on the bus (Fairclough 1986, 408). King's strategy of non-violent protest had worked.

Student sit-ins at lunch counters followed the bus boycott. Throughout the spring of 1960 sit-ins were taking place at lunch counters, movie theaters, department stores, libraries and churches throughout the South (Barksdale 1986, 30). These students followed the teaching Dr. King, turning the other cheek when struck. The images of young, black students in coats and ties getting dragged off stools, beaten by white crowds were shown around the country. The contrast between the two groups could not have been clearer. By the fall of 1960 the students had managed to integrate lunch counters in almost 100 cities throughout the South (Carson 1987, 451). Determined to keep the momentum, the students formed the Student Nonviolent Coordinating Committee (SNCC). SNCC was destined to become another key group in the African-American Civil Rights Movement.

Another non-violent protest group, the Congress of Racial Equality (CORE) was planning mass public resistance as well. After the Supreme Court declared segregated waiting rooms and restaurants illegal in December 1960 they organized a "Freedom Ride" from Washington, D.C. to New Orleans to high-light the ruling. On May 4, 1961 seven black and six white members of CORE boarded a bus. At each stop throughout the South the members used "white-only" waiting rooms together and ate at "white-only" restaurants together. The ride went as planned until the group reached Birmingham, Alabama. There the bus was attacked by a mob, burned, and group members beaten (The Fortieth Anniversary of the Freedom Ride 2001, 7). Despite the loss of their bus, the ride continued the next day, this time with 30 new members. The group was once again attacked in Montgomery and once again their ranks swelled. The spring and summer of 1961 saw hundreds of similar "Freedom Rides" throughout the South (McAdam 1983, 745). In the fall of that year the Interstate Commerce Commission declared any form of discrimination on busses, trains, and streetcars illegal. The non-violent tactics of the Civil Rights Movement had prevailed again.

The climax of the massive public resistance movement came on August 28, 1963. A quarter of million people marched on Washington D.C., down the National Mall to the Lincoln Memorial. Leaders from the NAACP, the National Urban League, and SNCC all spoke. Rosa Parks was introduced to the crowd (Reed 1999, 150). It was the last speaker of the day, however, who would capture the imagination of millions of Americans. On August 28, one hundred years after Abraham Lincoln issued the Emancipation Proclamation, Dr. Martin Luther King, Jr. appealing to the conscience of a nation, gave his famous "I have a Dream" speech on the steps of a memorial dedicated to the same Mister Lincoln; "When we let freedom ring from every village and every hamlet, from every state and every city, black men and white men, Jews and Gentiles, Protestant and Catholics, will be able to join hands and sing the words of the old Negro spiritual: Free at last, Free at last, Thank God Almighty, We are free at last (King 200, 121)."

Responding to growing public outcry and at the urging of President Kennedy and then President Johnson to take up the cause of African-American civil rights, Congress finally passed the Civil Rights Act of 1964 (Findlay 1990, 66). The Act banned discrimination in public places, employment practices, public places and increased the desegregation of schools. The next year Congress once again took up the cause and passed the Voting Rights Act of 1965 which gave back voting privileges to black Americans. The application of these Acts on the ground in the South took the influence and involvement of all the African-American civil rights organizations. SNCC and SCLC went to Alabama to register voters. CORE and the NAACP went to Mississippi to help desegregate it (Colaiaco 1986, 22).

Clashes between whites in favor of segregation and the Civil Rights Movement continued for the rest of the decade. Activists walked across the state of Mississippi in 1965 in a "march against fear (Sterling 1968, 222)." Along the way they registered over 4,000 new black voters. The leaders of the movement saw another legislative victory when Congress passed the Civil Rights Act of 1968 banning discrimination in housing (Leigh 1988, 158). The late sixties saw the Black Power movement, under the direction of SNCC leader H. Rapp Brown and Nation of Islam spokesman Malcolm Little (better known as Malcolm X), begin to gain power (Goldberg 1968, 120). There was a widening gulf between the groups over the proper response to continued white vigilante justice. The assassination of Dr. Martin Luther King, Jr. on April 4, 1968 marked the end of an era for the Civil Rights Movement. While the movement had some successes after Dr. King's death, most notably the renewal of the Voting Rights Act in 1970, the cohesion, coordination and sense of togetherness that had characterized the earlier African-American Civil Rights Movement was gone.

A Brief History of the Catholic Civil Rights Movement in Northern Ireland

The outbreak of violence in Northern Ireland in 1969 was not an isolated event. It occurred in the context of centuries of fractured relations between Protestants and Catholics. While some claim that the conflict dates from the 12th century[5], one of the key dates in the conflict is 1609. It was then that the British instituted a plan that called for creating "the Plantation of Ulster (Tonge 2002, 5)." The plan tried to attract settlers from all classes of British society to Ireland and pushed the native Irish off their land (Miller 1998, 46). The rules did not allow for settlers to even hire the native Irish to work their land. The result was that by 1700 less than 5 percent of Ulster was owned by Catholic Irish.

The victory of Protestant William of Orange in 1690 over Catholic James II ushered in another era of hostility between the two groups. As a result of William's victory an exclusively Protestant legislature was established in 1692 to run the whole of the island (Miller 1998, 49). What followed were a host of laws that relegated Catholics to second-class status; including a ban of Catholic ownership of arms, the exclusion of Catholics from the legal profession, and a ban on the Catholic purchase of land from Protestants amongst others. The main effect of the laws was to entrench the division between the Catholics and Protestants in Ireland. They added a political element to what had previously been a military conflict.

By the late 1700s, most of the laws had been taken off the books. Some of the laws applied to all citizens, such as the provision on buying land, and their application to

---

[5] This choice of dates is itself political. Catholics claim that problems began in 1609 with the plan for the Plantation of Ulster. Protestants claim the problems in Ulster arise before that with problems between warring Irish tribes, the Planters and Gaels.

Protestants became problematic. A rebellion in 1798 broke the relative calm. The failed rebellion is best known as being for Irish independence and as such was not strictly a Catholic uprising. In addition to the Catholic participants who were charged, 30 Protestant clergymen were also charged with treason for participating in the rebellion. The Act of Union in 1801 was a direct result of the failed rebellion. The Act abolished the independent Irish Parliament and formally made Ireland a part of the United Kingdom (Bric 2004, 17). Westminster now had direct control over the affairs of Ireland.

The next big conflict came in Belfast. Britain was expending a great deal of capital to industrialize Northern Ireland. As the place to find jobs, Belfast in particular, the cities of Northern Ireland began to see an influx of formally rural peasants. By 1835 the percentage of Catholics in Belfast had risen to 30 percent of the city's total population (Darby 1997, 23). The first signs of conflict for jobs and housing were being seen. The potato famine of the 1840s dramatically affected the counties of Ulster, albeit indirectly. The famine affected rural western and southern Ireland much more dramatically than the industrial north. As such, the economic differences between the two groups quickly found a political voice. Southern and western, mostly Catholic Ireland, organized a campaign to repeal the Act of Union and restore home rule. An equally strong voice developed in the north in favor of the Act and advocating a separate parliament in Ulster if the Act was repealed.

The rest of the 1800s saw a stiffening of the divide over Home Rule. By 1885, advocates against Home Rule had captured a majority of the seats assigned to Ulster in the British Parliament (Tonge 2002, 7). By 1905 the different factions against Home Rule had finally organized under the umbrella of the Ulster Unionist Council. It was from this group that the dominant Protestant political party, the Ulster Unionist Party, would emerge (Tonge 2002, 8).

At the same time, Home Rule forces who advocated for a legislative solution to the problem were organizing under the Irish Parliamentary party. The Irish Republican Brotherhood, the IRA and others continued to conduct revolutionary activities against British forces. While leaders of the Irish Parliamentary Party pushed the IRA as the alternative to their British counterparts if legislative efforts failed, they were unable to control the revolutionary groups. By 1912 Ireland was home to a full-blown civil war between the Catholic IRA and the Protestant Ulster Volunteer force (UVF); this despite the entire island still being under British control. After fighting in World War I, and with the public having no appetite for continuing to fight another war in Ireland, the British began the peace process (Cox 2000, 11). In 1920 the British Parliament passed the Government of Ireland Act of 1920 which partitioned the island into Southern and Northern Ireland. Each section was to have its own Parliament to deal with domestic matters, each was to send representatives to Westminster, and a Council of Ireland was to be created to deal with issues of common interest (Cox 2000, 10). In reality, only the northern section followed the terms of the act and the Council of Ireland never met. In 1921, Sinn Féin, the political arm of the IRA, and the British Government, signed the Anglo-Irish Agreement which created the Irish Free State. The agreement also included a provision allowing Northern Ireland to withdraw from the Irish Free State and remain a part of the United Kingdom which the Northern Ireland Parliament decided to take advantage of (Bric 2004, 8).

The parliament that was created in Northern Ireland consisted of a bicameral legislature. The government in Belfast was nominally subordinate to the national legislature in Westminster; however under the terms of the 1921 Anglo-Irish Agreement the Northern Ireland government had jurisdiction over the police, education policy, local government and social services. The only official authority that London maintained was the power to revoke legislative powers and dissolve parliament (Hennessey 2001, 3).

The two states began their existence in turmoil and violence. 232 people were killed and over 1,000 people were injured in Northern Ireland in 1922. This figure was not matched until 1972. As time passed, the government of Northern Ireland began creating institutions that excluded Catholics from power (Barton 1994, 9). Voting procedures were set-up to deny non-taxpayers the ability to vote and to give more than one vote to people who owned more than one property. The Protestant government used its monopoly over housing allocation and gerrymandering to create Protestant majority voting districts. This occurred most notably in Derry[6], a majority Catholic city that has continually elected Protestants (Hennessey 2001, 6). The police force that the government of Northern Ireland created was mostly Protestant; by the 1960's only 12 percent were Catholic (Darby 1991, 28). The education system favored Protestants as well, creating a state sponsored system of Protestant schools while forcing Catholics to fund up to half their education personally. Significant judicial powers were delegated to the Minister of Home Affairs, a Protestant patronage position. Catholics were discriminated against in public employment as well (Cameron Report 1969).

---

[6] The choice of names for Londonderry/Derry is another political decision. Catholics refer to it as Derry while Protestants use Londonderry. Derry is the term most commonly used by residents themselves and as such will be used for this study (Darby 1997, 28).

By making discrimination official government policy, the government in Northern Ireland had succeeded in consolidating the Catholic opposition. The worldwide depression of the 1930s saw an increase in sectarian violence. There were widespread riots in 1931, 1932, and 1935. In response Protestant and government leaders seized greater control. The exclusively Protestant police force received emergency powers to arrest anyone who they felt was a threat to the stability of the government (Anderson 2002, 23). As the economic situation improved violence did drop, but few leaders thought it had disappeared completely.

The economic boom of World War II and the post-war years created a better economic situation for Catholics. Outsiders with jobs came into Northern Ireland who did not yet have discriminatory policies in place. The government in Stormont relented slightly, making secondary education free for all citizens, Catholics and Protestants alike. The Catholic movement began to see their future in a Northern Ireland state, as opposed to a united Ireland (Barton 1994, 13). This newfound embrace of the Northern Ireland government can be seen in the failure of the IRA offensive from 1956-1962. As the IRA noted in their press release announcing the cessation of revolutionary activities, their failure was due to "attitude of the general public whose minds have been deliberately distracted from the supreme issues facing the Irish people – the unity and freedom of Ireland (Darby 1997, 31)."

The 1960s opened with optimism that the two sides in Northern Ireland truly could live together peacefully. In 1963, Terence O'Neil became Prime Minister promising to "build bridges between the two communities (O'Neil 1969, 23)." By 1965 Prime Ministers from Northern Ireland and the Republic of Ireland had exchanged visits for the first time. Protestants in the legislature were pushing back against this reconciliation. Unionist members picketed Parliament and paramilitary Protestant organizations killed Catholics (Barton 1994, 106). This action made no sense to Catholic leaders. The changes and programs Protestants were protesting were not significant and were not happening nearly fast enough. By 1969, it was clear that the more extreme branches of O'Neil's party were going to sabotage any chance at reform. On the Catholic side a peaceful Civil Rights Movement had developed, modeled after a similar campaign in the United States (White 1995, 333).

The 1969 marching season turned out to be a particularly violent one marking the start of the twenty-five year "Troubles." Protestant police attacked Catholics peacefully marching from Belfast to Derry in protest of housing rights. In August a march by Protestants through the Catholic section of Derry was attacked. The Protestant police force responded violently, leading the Irish Prime Minster, John Lynch, to declare: "we will not stand by (Elliot 1999, 319)." The violence quickly spread to Belfast. The Catholic region of Belfast was attacked by a Protestant mob while the police force stood aside. Seven people were killed and more than 3,000 were rendered homeless. By August 14, 1969 the British government realized it had to do something to prevent a full-scale war from breaking out; they sent troops to Derry and Belfast (Cox 2000, 11). While the initial reason given for the troop placement was to protect the Catholic population of both towns, it had the effect of being a symbol of repression: British troops on Irish soil. Despite the presence of British troops in Northern Ireland violence continued to flare up around the country.

35

In 1971, in a last-ditch effort to retain some semblance of control over the violence, the Northern Ireland government introduced a policy of internment. The police forces were given the ability to jail anyone they felt who might be treasonous against the Crown (Elliot 1999, 662). The policy failed miserably, merely entrenching Catholic opposition. The failure of the internment policy and the shooting deaths of 13 civilians by the British Army (Bloody Sunday) in 1972, led London to realize that the government of Northern Ireland had no control over the situation on the ground (and in the streets). In March 1972 they dissolved the Northern Ireland parliament (Elliot 1999, 605). Direct rule was imposed and from 1972 until the 1998 Good Friday accords, Northern Ireland was ruled by a Secretary of State for Northern Ireland appointed by Parliament in London.

AN INDEPENDENT JUDICIARY

The "third wave of democratization" ended up hitting Southeast Asia and South America the hardest. Some of the democracies did not develop as scholars predicated they would. For that reason the recent scholarly literature on the role of the judiciary in a democracy has focused on these countries. Examining why the judiciary was effective in some states in not others has led to conclusions about what role the judiciary must play if democracy is to succeed.

As Pilar Domingo noted in his study of the Supreme Court in Mexico, "judicial independence is a necessary and essential aspect of democratic accountability (Domingo 2000, 705)." Judicial independence means that the judicial branch has the power of judicial review, judges can make decisions free from political considerations and the judicial branch gets to decide what cases it hears (Iaryczower 2002, 699). Independence can be written into the constitution; however, the independent nature of the judiciary is only resolved through the interpretation and application of the constitution. What is the relationship between the judiciary and the other branches of government? Can the judiciary review the legality of legislative acts? Should judges be free from public pressure or amendable to the will of the people? The answers to these questions shape the role of the judicial body.

The first duty of an independent judiciary is to protect the rule of law and provide checks and balances against the instruments of the state; in essence provide judicial review. As Raymond Duncan wrote, "Presidential decree and state-of-siege powers [seized by the legislature] can make a mockery out of the judicial system (Duncan 1976, 152)." Secondly, they should provide justice for all citizens by protecting individual rights from overzealous legislators and executives. Having the rights of citizens written in to the constitution does not in and of itself assure citizens of those rights. The judiciary must be able to protect those rights if the will of a majoritarian government is to be regulated on behalf of minorities (Domingo 2000, 705). The independence of the judiciary is essential in conducting these tasks. Without it, due process and impartiality cannot be assured.

An independent judiciary will have judges who are politically independent. This will allow judges to make judicial decisions without fear of external political pressure and short-term considerations. They also need to be protected from undue influence exerted by parties who have business before the court. Bribery, cultural and ethnic bonds can all lead to unfair rulings. They should also be protected from certain democratic influences. Majority opinion, mass media coverage, and public visibility can all influence judges to make decisions that are not in the interests of all citizens (Verner 1984, 463). Decisions must be based on the rule of law and "not simply echo the views of the government of the day," as Richard Rose succinctly put it (Rose 1976, 255).

There are ways to ensure the independence of judges. The first is by using an appointment process. Appointing, rather than electing judges insulates jurists from the shifting winds of majority opinion. While this might make them beholden to other actors for their power, the decisions judges use that power to make remain independent. Second, appointing judges for life shields them from the pressures of the policy-makers who appoint them to the bench. This creates a situation "where judicial appointments are made for life [and] judicial decisions are freer than if the judge has to consider what the effect of his decision will be on his chances for reappointment or for re-election by the legislature (Needler 1968, 154)." These two steps help minimize the possibility of the court being subjugated to other branches of government.

The independence of judges is not the only key to an independent judiciary. The scope of the powers of judicial review that a court possesses is also important. It allows the judicial branch to review the activities of other branches to determine their legality. A judiciary with limited powers of review will remain subordinate to the whims and intentions of the other branches. Additionally as Arpad Von Lazar notes, a judiciary that is not independent cannot take full advantage of the powers of review they do possess because "political considerations prevent them from applying this power (Von Lazar 1971, 40)."

It must be noted that it does not matter where the judicial branch gets its power. George Lovell and Michael McCain argue that the idea of judicial independence is "highly misleading (Wolbrecht 2005, 258)." The power of the judiciary is determined by "actors in other branches (Wolbrecht 2005, 262)," and therefore it is not independent. The judiciary serves as a convenient dumping ground for decisions the other two branches do not want to make. Legislators pass along responsibility for decisions in highly political cases to the judicial branch when they expect them to rule in a certain manner, thus undermining the independence of the judiciary. However, as Von Lazar points out, it does not matter in determining judicial independence how the courts rule, but merely that they get to rule. The judiciary is not independent when the legislative and executive branches can pass what are traditional judicial issues to ad-hoc committees, investigatory commissions and use other means of by-passing the judicial branch (Von Lazar 1971, 155). As Matías Iaryczower notes in his review of judicial independence in

Argentina, it does not matter if justices want to challenge the president or the legislature, merely that they can challenge them (Iaryczower 2002, 699).

Some scholars, most notably Gerald Rosenberg, say that the courts themselves are ineffective agents of change. He argues that courts are only able to bring about reform if the marketplace or other actors provide incentives to comply. He concludes "that at best [the courts] can second the social reform acts of other branches of government...A court's [role] is akin to officially recognizing the evolving state of affairs (Rosenberg 1991, 338)." Rosenberg applies this thesis to the American Civil Rights movement, most notably the *Brown v. Board of Education* decision. There is a problem with Rosenberg's view of causation. His path of causation assumes that social change is only caused by court cases when there is no other possible influence. He dismisses some court decisions arguing that the court simply reflected real life events already occurring. As the delay between the *Brown* decision and its implementation shows, the real world was definitely not desegregating on its own. Other court decisions are dismissed based on the length of time between the decision and its implementation. Once again we can look at the *Brown* decision and find that it was the *Brown II* ruling that caused the federal government to take up the case of school desegregation (Russo 1994, 297). The leaders of the Civil Rights Movement were trying to push all levers of power at the same time, so as Kim Scheppele notes "with his strict picture of what would count as causation, it's not surprising that he [Rosenberg] find little influence of the court in any area of social policy (Scheppele 1992, 466)." It is hard to untangle the efforts of social movements to appeal to the court and to the federal government. As in the case of school integration, they were often complimentary actions. Additionally, the gains seen by the American Civil

Rights Movement were the accomplishment of many different forces advocating for change at the same time. The process by which Rosenberg measures causation is not very well suited to explaining these complex interactions. Another problem with Rosenberg's conclusion is that he never considers counterfactuals. It is difficult to determine whether or not the court was the cause of social change if one does not examine what would have happened if the court had not ruled. Rosenberg would have done well to examine President Eisenhower's personal responses in the "Little Rock Nine" case in which he states that he will "use the full power of the U.S., whatever force may be necessary to prevent obstruction of the laws and to carry out the orders of the federal court" (Calloway-Thomas 1996, 627). It is tough to argue that the court decision had no influence on the social change that took place. While Rosenberg does raise an important point, "What happens after the decision?" it should not diminish the importance of the decision itself as an impetus for change.

How does an independent judiciary, one with the power of judicial review, encourage leaders of social movements to choose a strategy of assimilation? If courts are not subject to the same majoritarian pressures that the legislative and executive branches are, they can serve as an avenue of last resort for groups that are continually discriminated against by the other two branches of government (Moog 1998, 410). Individuals can bring suits seeking redress and are not dependent on the decisions of discriminatory government officials. It provides opportunities to influence the policy making process for groups who might otherwise not be able to. This is especially helpful to minorities whose interests are often in direct conflict with the ruling majority class. The power of the court rests in the paradox that minorities must by definition lose elections in first-past-the-post elections; however, in a court of law the claims of those same minorities are given equal consideration. This connection is made explicitly clear in Alison Brysk's study of human rights in post-authoritarian Argentina. For her, the protection of human rights for all citizens, minority and majority, by the judiciary is the ultimate sign that judiciary has ascended to its proper role in a democracy (Brysk 1994).

In systems that do not possess an independent judiciary, it is most often the executive branch that has control over the judicial branch (Nova 1976, 115). The court is subservient to the will of the executive and plays almost no role in the political process. The executive branch determines the legality of legislation and has a preponderance of power. When the judicial branch is not independent, the executive branch becomes responsible for creating the rule of law (Dua 1983, 464). It is the executive, not the judiciary who decides when civil rights should be protected. Essentially the executive branch takes over the power of judicial review. This is a problematic relationship since the executive is elected and responsive to a majority who often have very little interest in protecting the rights of those not in the majority.

If the executive has enough control over the judicial branch, the courts serve simply as another venue to deal with political disputes. Dissidents that cannot be defeated at the ballot box are defeated in court (Magalhães 1999, 44). It can also be used in the rare cases where the executive does not prevail on a policy issue. The action of the legislative branch can simply be declared unconstitutional. This arrangement prevents policy disputes from being decided by the citizenry.

When the judicial branch is not independent, when it does not possess the power of judicial review, it limits the opportunities for groups, such as social movements, to seek redress. The ruling elite and the policies they decide cannot be challenged. The courts are no threat to the current power structure, and hence no threat to the current ruling elite. Minority rights are not protected, and since they lack the ability to review actions of other branches of government the court is not a place to seek redress for discriminatory policies. Political systems that do not have independent judiciaries with the power of judicial review encourage leaders to pursue confrontational strategies that attempt to change the existing system. The system cannot answer their demands and therefore the system itself must be changed.

THE ROLE OF THE JUDICIARY IN THE CIVIL RIGHTS MOVEMENT IN THE UNITED STATES AND NORTHERN IRELAND

The judicial system in the United States does not confine itself to statutory interpretation; it also has the power of judicial review (Huntington 1968, 112). This power was established early in the 1800's with the *Marbury v. Madison* Supreme Court Case (Ellis 1971). Because the courts can review action taken by the legislature and the executive, including Southern State Legislatures and Governors, the leaders of the African-American Civil Rights movement were encouraged to pursue a strategy of working within the existing system to achieve change. The court became a guardian of minority rights.

Since 1938 and the *Missouri v. Canada* ruling which upheld the equality of blacks, the Supreme Court in the United States has served as a guardian of the civil rights of minorities (Agyeman 1991). Their rulings regarding segregation, school desegregation, voting rights and reapportionment served as an impetuous for societal revolutions. In the words of Judge Irving Kaufman, the court became "an accelerator of governmental activity rather than a brake" (O'Brien 1985, 35). Using its power of judicial review, the court stepped in and corrected socioeconomic and political inequalities. Judicial review served the purpose it purported to: it provided an avenue for the Civil Rights Movement to challenge policy.

The leaders of the American Civil Rights Movement recognized this possibility early on. The National Association for the Advancement of Colored People (NAACP) was one of the first organizations to use the courts to advance the cause of the Civil Rights Movement. Harry T. Moore, executive director of the NAACP in Florida said that the goal of the NAACP was "achieving a full program of civil rights for Negro citizens" (Miller 2000, 216). Recognizing that the courts were constitutionally obliged to defend equal rights, the NAACP, under the direction of Moore, filed suit to require local school boards to provide equal pay for black teachers. This was one of many cases in which the NAACP used the courts to advance their case for equal rights.

The NAACP also recognized that in order to advance their case through the electorate they needed to change Southern voting laws. The NAACP used the courts to their advantage. They asked the court to grant Southern blacks their rights as federal citizens, as guaranteed in the Constitution. Using the courts to advance their claims to civil rights was not a challenge to the system, it was just the opposite, it was using the power of judicial review to challenge illegal activity.

Working with Civil Rights leaders in Texas, the NAACP appealed to the Supreme Court in 1927, arguing against the constitutionality of "white primary laws." This was a deliberate choice by the NAACP leadership (Hine 1977, 45). They realized that they could not win this battle at the ballot box. After several appeals, decisions, and changes by the Texas legislature the NAACP finally won the battle against "white primary laws" in 1944 when the U.S. Supreme Court declared all-white primaries to be illegal. While the idea was still widely unpopular amongst the majority of voters, the NAACP strategy of asking the judiciary to affirm their constitutionally guaranteed rights had worked.

The Civil Rights Movement achieved some of its most important progress through the Supreme Court: *Missouri v. Canada (1938)* made law the belief in the unconditional equality of blacks; *Smith v. Allwright (1944)* made all white primaries illegal; *Brown v. Board of Education (1954)* declared that "separate was inherently unequal," and made segregation illegal; *Heart of Atlanta Model Inc. v. United States (1961)* made private discrimination illegal in public accommodations; and *Griggs v. Duke Power Company (1971)* made companies responsible for hiring and firing practices which caused the exclusion of minorities from the workplace. Having seen first hand the redress of their injustices by the U.S. Supreme Court, the leaders of the Civil Rights movement continued to pursue a strategy of working through the system. Judicial review was helping them achieve their goals; there was no need to try and destroy the system. As one member of the Montgomery Boycott proclaimed, "Praise the Lord. God Almighty has spoken from Washington, D.C. (Sterling 1968, 7)."

The judicial system in Northern Ireland did not have the power of judicial review. Unable to have discriminatory laws overturned through appeals to the judicial branch, leaders of the Catholic Civil Rights Movement were encouraged to pursue other means of overturning the laws. The result was a violent attempt to change policy.

There were three levels to the court system in Northern Ireland (see figure 3). The first stop was the Belfast Crown Court (Anderson 2002, 56). Decisions could then be appealed to the Court of Appeal for Northern Ireland. Finally, decisions could be appealed to the British House of Lords, which functioned as the court of last resort for the United Kingdom (Anderson 2002, 63). While he had no jurisdiction over court decisions, the Northern Ireland Minister of Home Affairs could commute sentences for individuals convicted in Belfast.

The Northern Ireland Judicial System 1922-1972

Belfast Crown Court

↓

Court of Appeals for Northern Ireland

↓

House of Lords, The Court of Last Resort for the United Kingdom

The Northern Ireland Minister of Home Affairs could commute sentences for individuals convicted in Belfast.

Figure 3

The power of judicial review did not exist in Northern Ireland. Because of this situation, Catholics in Northern Ireland had no place to appeal discriminatory laws and rulings from the legislature.

The problem with appealing to the courts in Northern Ireland was that Parliament, not the judiciary, was the ultimate arbiter of rights. The courts simply ruled on whether or not activity was in accord with the relevant law (Tonge 2002, 20). They did not have the authority to rule on the constitutionality of laws themselves. If a majority wanted to curtail the rights of minorities, as in 1969 when a law was passed that allowed suspected Republicans to be held indefinitely without trial, legally it could be done if the rule was passed in a lawfully manner (Anderson 2002, 51). And in practice this was often the case, the legislature would pass laws limiting the rights of Catholics and then the police would enforce those laws. As long as the police were enforcing laws that had legitimately passed the legislature, the courts were forced to rule the discriminatory action legal (Narain 1975, 43). This process limited the rights of both Catholics and Protestants to apply to the courts for redress of grievances; Catholics were far more likely

47

however, to have grievances. The leaders of the Catholic Civil Rights movement were unable to get the court to review the actions of the legislature and they could not win seats in the legislature, so they were encouraged to pursue a strategy of working outside the system to achieve any change.

In 1967, a Catholic group from Northern Ireland, the Campaign for Social Justice, attempted to bring their push for minority rights to the courts. A protest was lodged against the Special Powers Act passed by Parliament. The law made "Republican[7] clubs or any like organization however described" (Rose 1976, 277) illegal. The case worked its way through the legal system with the British House of Lords finally concluding that act was in fact lawful because it had been passed using proper procedures. While the ruling was expected given the judicial climate in Northern Ireland, in the words of two Protestant writers "it was the final proof to the minority community that they could expect no aid from Britain in their struggle for what they regarded as their legitimate civil rights (Hadden 1973, 13)."

Even when the courts in Northern Ireland did manage to rule in favor of minority rights, the executive could and often did overrule the decision of the court. In some cases the government simply retroactively applied legislation to legalize action already taken (Narain 1975, 235).

In Northern Ireland the majority ruled the executive and legislative branches of government. The judicial branch did not possess the ability to declare the actions of the other two branches illegal. The political system in Northern Ireland, which did not have judicial review, did not provide a way for the leaders of the Catholic Civil Rights

---

[7] In Northern Ireland a "republican" refers not to a political ideology, but to a Catholic. This term is used because it is often thought that all Catholics wish to reunite with the Republic of Ireland, which is majority Catholic.

movement to achieve their goals. The leaders, in order to meet the goals of their members, were forced to confront the system itself and achieve redress by changing the very structure of the system itself.

ELECTABLE IDEOLOGIES

Judicial challenges are not the only mechanism in place for social movements to achieve change. The electoral process is another way to influence policy. Elections are the main way that democracies provide a government "for the people, by the people." In most democracies, elections serve to create a government for the majority of the people. By their very definition, these types of government create problems for minority groups.

A policy of "one man, one vote" does not necessarily deprive minorities of their electoral influence. There are strategies that can increase the number of electable ideologies on the ballot. The first is that social movements can partner with other groups in order to achieve a majority. The downside to this proposition is that the groups must bargain away some of their own beliefs in order to make the coalition work. The second way social movements that are composed of minorities can achieve power is systemic. Communal electoral roles can be guaranteed constitutionally so that the votes of different groups are counted separately. This ensures that social movements can elect their own representatives regardless of their minority status (Steiner 1969, 296). However, the majority of the mechanisms by which minority social movements can assert electoral influence are conditional, rather than structural. They only work if systemic conditions are correct.

An electable ideology is a set of beliefs and ideas that a candidate possesses and he or she can get elected to public office holding those beliefs. Being an electable ideology is not about who can run for office, but who can win office. It is not simply an argument for pluralism because it is not about the number of views tolerated by society. It is an argument about the number of different parties that can win elections. A view may be tolerated and allowed to exist by the state, but that does not mean it has enough support to win an election somewhere in the state. In Northern Ireland Catholics were allowed to exist. Catholicism was simply not an electable ideology.

The more electable ideologies there are in a political system, the more likely it is that social movements will use elections and work within the system to achieve change. An environment in which there are numerous electable ideologies means that there is a possibility that alternative ideas and policies can get a place in government. The more legitimately electable candidates that exist in an election, the more fragmented the majority becomes and the better the chance groups currently outside the majority have of getting elected.

In a political system that does not have more than one electable ideology, only a small range of views are present in government. With regards to elections, it means that candidates who possess views that are not held by the majority cannot get elected anywhere in the political system. In this type of system the majority holds a monopoly on political power.

This type of political system has a dramatic effect on the strategy chosen by leaders of social movements. If they have problems with their current situation, they cannot change the situation through elections. It encourages leaders to work outside the system rather than through it. Change has to come through violence and the destruction of the current system. Once citizens feel that there is no possibility of recourse for their concerns at the ballot box, they will often seek recourse at the point of a gun.

HOW THE NUMBER OF ELECTABLE IDEOLOGIES INFLUENCE SOCIAL MOVEMENT
STRATEGY IN THE UNITED STATES AND NORTHERN IRELAND

There are four conditions that must be met in order for a government to be "for the people, by the people:" (Rose 1976, 253)

1. Citizens must be voting for offices that have the ability to make politically important decisions.
2. Citizens must be able to choose from more than one candidate.
3. Citizens must be able to vote without fear of intimidation or retaliation.
4. The votes of citizens must be honestly counted.

Elections take place in countries around the world that are not considered democracies. In the last Iraqi election before the United States invasion, Saddam Hussein won with 100% of the vote (BBC News 2002). While the conditions above do not cause electable ideologies, for the election of those ideologies to have any effect on governing, these conditions must be present. These conditions were present for blacks outside the South in the United States and for Catholics in Northern Ireland when the Civil Rights Movements were organizing. However, in Northern Ireland these conditions led to the repression of the Catholic minority. Because a candidate with views favorable to the minority Catholics could not win an election anywhere in the country, leaders of the Catholic Civil Rights Movement were encouraged to pursue strategies outside the existing electoral system. In the United States, where it was possible to elect candidates with views favorable to African-Americans, leaders of the American Civil Rights Movement were encouraged to use the existing electoral system to produce the changes they hoped for.

The political structure in Northern Ireland can be broken down into two and only two communities since the separation with the Republic of Ireland occurred in 1921. The two communities are known by the religion of the members: Protestants and Catholics. The system that existed in Northern Ireland during the emergence of the civil rights movement in the 1950s, 60s and 70s was "castelike" (Harris 1972). A single attribute, religion, immediately placed someone into one of these two communities. Once placed in a community it was virtually impossible to escape. First off, it is not a simple matter to change one's religion. And secondly, in Northern Ireland, even if you changed your religion, you simply became an "ex-Catholic" (Rose 1976, 265). Once you were a member of the community, you were a member for life.

In Northern Ireland, elections have always meant one thing for Catholic candidates, defeat. This is because the group in the majority, the Protestants, has been a cohesive voting block in the six northern counties since the 1921 separation. By simply exercising their right to vote, Protestants maintained a monopoly on political power. Protestantism was the only electable ideology. Catholicism was not an electable ideology in Northern Ireland (Rose 1971, 462). Possessing the majority allowed Protestants to govern Northern Ireland without any checks and balances. The structural arraignment that existed offered the party that won the majority of seats in parliament control of both the legislature and the executive. Unlike the American South, Protestants did not to place any formal restrictions on Catholic voting rights. Due to gerrymandering and pure demographic characteristics there was no need to form a ruling coalition. Catholics were not asked to give their consent to the government they existed under (Barritt 1962).

The selection system used by Protestants excluded Catholic candidates from the election process. Protestant candidates had a built in majority; they were never required nor did they need to reach out to the Catholic minority to get elected. In fact, Protestant candidates who did, such as Terence O'Neil, risked the support of the majority for reaching out to Catholics (Elliot 1998, 379). They were either defeated elections or did not find themselves a candidate the next time around.

Factionalism had a short shelf life in Northern Ireland. Out of necessity, Protestants responded to differences in opinion by coming together. Their leaders recognized that if they did not, the Catholic minority voting in a bloc, might be elected to arbitrate between the two. The result of all this systemic pressure on the Catholic minority was that Ulster Unionist Party[8] held a majority of the seats in parliament from its creation in 1921 until the government was dissolved by Britain 1972. They won this majority in elections that were free and fair. Ulster and the Protestants always won because of demographics; they made up 65% of the population (Rose 1971, 261).

Since Catholic candidates could not win election anywhere in Northern Ireland the leaders of the Civil Rights Movement were prevented from challenging the Protestants' hold on power through elections. They were at the electoral will of the majority with no way to work through the system to achieve change. There was no electable ideology that was friendly to their cause. Leaders of the Catholic Civil Rights movement in Northern Ireland looked at this situation and decided to confront the system itself. They were unable to achieve change at the ballot box and thus pursued change through violence. It was a way to confront the Protestant majority.

There were significant differences between the nature of the political system in Northern Ireland and the one in the United States. In Northern Ireland, the Protestant majority did not need support from Great Britain to rule. The political structure allowed them able to manage their own internal affairs with only minimal support from

[8] The Ulster Union Party was the dominant Protestant party in Northern Ireland politics.

Westminster. Leaders of the African-American Civil Rights Movement in the United States recognized that they could not use elections to pursue change in the South. It was simply a matter of demographics; there were more whites than blacks in the South (The Washington Research Project 1972, 13). However, unlike in Northern Ireland, the Southern delegation did not hold sway over the entire electorate. While it was impossible to elect candidates who were friendly to the cause of black Civil Rights in the South, it was possible and often occurred in other parts of the United States. Advocacy for black Civil Rights was an electable ideology in places in the United States, mostly notably the North. Local government leaders in the South needed the support of the national government to continue governing, be it through funding or other levers of persuasion. Electing a desegregationist anywhere in the United States had a measurable effect on the lives of blacks in the South. As Martin Luther King Jr. said in 1957, "Give us the ballot and we will bring this nation to a new society based on justice and dedicated to peace (Hamilton 1973, 43)."

Leaders of the African-American Civil Rights Movement recognized that influences from outside the South might be able to help them inside the South. In the South blacks were the minority; the South, however was part of a larger political entity, the United States. While they had been historically ignored by national politicians in Washington, D.C. the "Great Migration" during World War II gave blacks an influential electoral voice in states outside the South. The rest of the country did not have the same cohesive voting bloc that whites in the South did. Because of this, by voting in a bloc, blacks could use their vote to change elections outside of the South. They had left the fields of the South for the factories of the North. They came for better jobs and ended up with increased political rights.

John F. Kennedy was one of the first national politicians to appeal to leaders of the black civil rights movement for support. In the 1960 presidential election, an astounding seventy-two percent of blacks voted Democratic. Accounting for seven percent of the total Democratic vote, blacks managed to push Kennedy to victory. In an election in which the white vote was almost evenly spilt between Republicans and Democrats, the black vote decided who won (Alexrod 1974, 718). As a result, when Kennedy entered office he was ready and willing to respond to the calls of those same Civil Rights leaders for expanded rights.

These feelings on segregation and civil rights were not universal. In the South, politicians lined up to publicly denounce the courts and the federal government. Alabama Governor George Wallace even managed to mount a somewhat successful presidential campaign based almost entirely on his opposition to desegregation. Despite Wallace's Southern appeal, tireless campaigning, and lifelong membership in the Democratic Party, who included Dixiecrats opposed to desegregation, Democrats did not make him their nominee for president. Politicians who supported the positions of the black civil rights leaders, many who owed their jobs to them, no longer found it politically expedient to support segregationist candidates. Running as an independent in the 1968 election, Governor Wallace managed to carry five southern states. The truly interesting part for Civil Rights leaders was that Governor Wallace's presidential campaign took place against the backdrop of the Voting Rights Acts of 1960 and 1965 which significantly expanded the rights of African-Americans in the United States. The

Voting Rights Acts had a significant effect on number of blacks registered to vote in South. While this may have been an instance of the federal government using its position of supremacy to force policy on the states, the Acts had to be enacted by elected officials from each state. The time period from 1960-1971 saw an increase in the number of blacks registered to vote from 485,000 to 1,666,000. More than half of blacks of voting age in the South were now registered voters (Government Printing Office 1971, Table 701).

Some scholars have argued that the expansion of black voting rights was the result of Cold War morality on the part of the United States government (Skrentny 1998, 242). While this may have contributed to eagerness of the federal government to embrace civil rights reform, the initial push came from other sources. The Court declared segregation illegal before President Eisenhower made it federal policy. Additionally, survey data from the 1940s and 1905s show that "white racial attitudes were moving in a clearly liberal direction... aided by the Courts (Schuman 2003, 435)," and demonstrated by the electorate. Change had occurred through elections and further change could be achieved in the same manner.

Comparing George Wallace's campaign for governor of Alabama to Kennedy's campaign for President, both of whom won, shows that in the United States numerous ideologies were electable. Candidates advocating segregationist policies did not have a monopoly on political power. Elected politicians represented all stripes of life. There were Democrats, Republicans, segregationists, desegregations, conservatives, liberals, and centrists in Congress. Black Civil Rights leaders recognized that they need not get politicians friendly to their cause elected in the South; they simply had to get them elected somewhere. All it takes is one Senator or Representative to introduce a bill. Because advocacy for black Civil Rights was an electable ideology in certain places within the United States the leaders of the black Civil Rights Movement were encouraged to work through the existing system. Their efforts showed that elections in the U.S. could be positive agents of change for their movements.

THE FEDERAL SYSTEM OF GOVERNMENT

Federalism is the division of the authority between national and local governments (Bickers 2001, 142). It does not have an exact form. There are symmetric and asymmetric relationships. A symmetric relationship is one in which the different levels of governmental authority share equally in the condition and solution to problems in the political system. In an asymmetric relationship the different levels of government do not share responsibility equally (Tarlton 1965, 861). No matter if it is asymmetric or symmetric, all federal political systems share one common characteristic: political power is shared in some manner (Corwin 1950).

There are benefits for social movements that exist in political systems in which the national government is supreme. In countries with federal structures, different view points have an opportunity for political expression within the system as a whole, at both local and national levels. If the national government is supreme they can provide oversight and protection to citizens from discriminatory local rules and laws (Tarlton 1965, 872). This system of organizing government encourages the leaders of social movements that develop to pursue strategies of assimilation. Social movements can make appeals to local officials and if those fail, national officials have the power to override local officials and meet the needs of social movements. By working through the existing political structure, social movements in federal systems with a dominant national government can achieve their goals.

A federal system of government in which the national government is supreme is not the only model for organizing democratic society. There are systems in which power is not shared between the national and local governments. Several democracies have systems in which most power is consolidated in the hands of local government. This is often the situation in cases where the composition of the population creates problems for effective governing at a national level. If power is consolidated at the national level different groups from around the country would be in continuous conflict. These type of systems create far fewer opportunities to influence policy. If social movements are unable to appeal to the national elite to help them achieve their goals, they are often left without recourse if denied by local officials. Political systems in which the national government is not supreme encourage leaders to pursue a strategy of confrontation because they have no avenue of appeal for local decisions. The best way to achieve their goals is not to work through the system, but to change the system itself.

THE NATURE OF GOVERNMENT AND THE CIVIL RIGHTS MOVEMENT IN THE UNITED STATES AND NORTHERN IRELAND

The United States has a federal system of government. The power to make policy is shared between local, state and national governments. The federal relationship in the United States is not a symmetric one however. Engrained in the Constitution and affirmed by the Supreme Court, the national government has risen to become the predominant power nowadays. In rulings throughout the years, the Supreme Court has continually increased the power of the nation government stating that they have the ultimate authority in protecting the civil rights enshrined in the Constitution and Bill of Rights. It is this system of government, one in which the national government has a preponderance of power, in which the U.S. Civil Rights movement worked.

The changing nature of the federal system in the United States was extremely useful to the Civil Rights Movement. Prior to the New Deal, federalism in the United States existed as "layer cake federalism (Bickers 2001, 142)." There were clear divisions between the duties of the national government and the duties of state governments. These duties were unique to each level of government and did not overlap. The center of politics in American life at this time resided at the state level. The most important policy debates were not occurring in Washington, but in state capitols.

The New Deal and President Roosevelt ushered in a new age of federalism, "picket-fence federalism (Bickers 2001, 147)." In this model, policy was made at the national level but utilized state and local governments to implement the policies. The policy making process was now top-down. The national government in Washington D.C. ascended to power over state governments. This change in the dynamics of federalism, to

61

a system in the national government was the most powerful, was extremely helpful to the African-American Civil Rights movement. The leaders of the movement were operating in a system where the national government could overrule the discriminatory policies of the state governments, and as such were encouraged to pursue a strategy of working through the system (and with the national government) to achieve their goals.

The 1950s and 60s were an interesting time for the leaders of the African-American Civil Rights Movement. They were seeing gains in equality on paper through Supreme Court rulings; however, in reality blacks were not seeing changes in their personal situation. The Court had told them they had certain rights, to vote in democratic primaries or attend all-white schools, for example, but in truth they could not utilize those rights. The *Brown v. Board of Education* ruling is a good example of this. Many southern school districts, rather than abide by the Court's ruling, "separate is inherently unequal," simply shut down their school systems (Brookover 1993, 163). Others simply ignored the ruling, necessitating the *Brown II* decision (Russo 1994, 297). Recognizing that solutions to their problems could not be found at the state level, leaders of the movement appealed to the national government for application of the rights the Court confirmed that they had (Calloway-Thomas 1996, 626).

One area in which the national government was particularly active was school integration. Little Rock, Arkansas became the test case for how far the national government was willing to go in addressing the civil rights demands of social movements. Arkansas Governor Oval Fabus had responded to the *Brown* decision by saying, "It is evident to me that Arkansas is not ready for a complete and sudden mixing of the races in the public school" (Bates 1962, 48). The NAACP leadership recognized the limitations of waiting for a Southern governor up for re-election to comply with the widely unpopular ruling. In 1956, Wiley Barton, state chairman of the Legal Defense Committee of the NAACP, filed suit in federal court to force the school system in Little Rock to integrate. The federal judge ordered that desegregation had to occur immediately and nine students were selected to attend Central High in Little Rock on the first day of school September 4, 1957. Governor Fabus, relishing the opportunity to secure the support of the conservative branch of the Democratic Party, called up the Arkansas National Guard to prevent the "Little Rock Nine" from entering the school. The students once again tried to attend school on September 23 and once again the National Guard, on Governor Fabus's orders, prevented them from attending Central.

It was at this point the leaders of the Civil Rights movement in Arkansas utilized the national government's supremacy to advance their case. Daisy Bates, the chair of the state NAACP organization, sent President Eisenhower a personal telegram stating that they were "standing steadfast with our community's compliance with the law – both local and federal." The telegram ended with Ms. Bates appealing to President Eisenhower for all the support he could give and "to which our free American society is entitled" (Calloway-Thomas 1996, 626). President Eisenhower recognized that the denial of rights guaranteed by the Constitution and affirmed by the courts was an affront not only to democracy, but to the supremacy of the national government also. Writing back he said "the law cannot be flouted with impunity by any individual or mob of extremists" and that he would "use the full power of the U.S., whatever force may be necessary to prevent obstruction of the laws and to carry out the orders of the federal court" (Calloway-Thomas 1996, 627). To that end he nationalized the Arkansas National Guard and ordered them to stand down. He then deployed elements of the 101st Airborne Division to protect the students. Civil Rights leaders had used the national government to achieve their goal.

This appeal to national officials was only possible because of the dominant position of the national government in the United States. Leaders of the Civil Rights Movement recognized that using the existing political system was an effective way of achieving redress for their demands. It was a highly successful strategy that they utilized early and often. In 1960, President Eisenhower, at the request of the NAACP leadership, once again utilized national resources, this time US Marshals, to integrate the University of Mississippi. Civil Rights leaders had found that the federal structure in which a friendly national government was supreme encouraged them to work through the existing system.

The nature of the political system in Northern Ireland was completely different. The national government of the United Kingdom had almost no power over the local Northern Ireland government. Since no means existed for the leaders of the Catholic Civil Rights movement to appeal to the national government under the current system, they were encouraged to pursue strategies that destroyed the system to meet their goals.

An interesting relationship existed between Great Britain and Northern Ireland since the split with the Republic of Ireland in 1921. When it existed from 1921 to 1972 the Northern Ireland Parliament in Stormont had complete governing authority. A bicameral parliament existed in which the fifty-two seat House of Commons was elected by a straight vote in the Protestant gerrymandered districts. A twenty-six seat Senate existed as the upper-house, of which twenty-four were selected by a PR system by the

House of Commons, which was entirely Protestant.[9] The Senate could not propose legislation, simply possessing delaying power similar to the House of Lords at Westminster. However, since the Senate was selected by the completely Protestant House of Commons they were merely a rubberstamp for policy. The British policy at this time was mostly one of disinterest. The Home Secretary appointed by the Prime Minster for the United Kingdom who was responsible for managing the day to day affairs of Northern Ireland, was also responsible for licensing London taxi cabs. The Parliament in Westminster only had responsibility over foreign trade, national defense, customs and excise, and major taxes with regard to Northern Ireland (see figure 4). Every other policy area was the purview of the Northern Ireland Parliament in Stormont. It was not possibly for any member of Westminster to raise a question which was within the purview of the Prime Minister of Northern Ireland (Elliot 2002, 663). London did possess the power to dissolve the Northern Ireland Parliament. They had no official influence over local policies, the selection of cabinet ministers, or even security plans (see figure 4). During this time, since the Ulster party never lost an election and therefore did not have to worry about defections, the Prime Minister of Northern Ireland, as selected by Parliament in Stormont had almost most absolute control over the affairs of Northern Ireland. (Fisk 1975).

---

[9] While the Ulster Party never lost an election in Northern Ireland it was not the only Protestant party that existed in Parliament. Up until its dissolution in 1972, no Catholic ever held a seat in either house in Parliament.

The Government of Northern Ireland 1921-1972

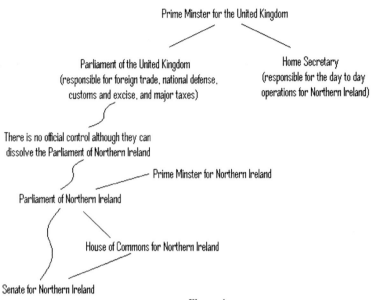

Prime Minister for the United Kingdom

Parliament of the United Kingdom
(responsible for foreign trade, national defense,
customs and excise, and major taxes)

Home Secretary
(responsible for the day to day
operations for Northern Ireland)

There is no official control although they can
dissolve the Parliament of Northern Ireland

Prime Minster for Northern Ireland

Parliament of Northern Ireland

House of Commons for Northern Ireland

Senate for Northern Ireland

Figure 4

Every attempt by Catholic leaders to appeal to Westminster was defeated by "convention," which prevented discussion of any issues that were under the purview of the Northern Ireland Parliament (Hennessey 2001, 6). It required a real parliamentary genius to be able to get discussion regarding Northern Ireland in Westminster. It was not until the 1972 riots that London even placed the "nuclear option" on the table. After dissolving the Northern Ireland Parliament, London appointed a Secretary of State for Northern Ireland who had complete control over both the political system and the security apparatus (Rose 1976, 279). This unique arraignment created a political system in which very few people had the authority to change or direct policy. From 1921 until 1972 when Parliament was suspended, the Prime Minister had a monopoly on political power; the national government of the United Kingdom could not make policy for

Northern Ireland. Leaders of the Catholic Civil Rights Movement did not have many avenues to appeal to (Rose 1976, 278). The system had consolidated all power in the hands of the executive, the Prime Minister of Northern Ireland. Unlike the United States there was no national government to appeal to. It was not a vast bureaucracy that had jurisdiction over public housing, employment rules, civil rights commissions; it was the Prime Minister (Nelson 1984). The local MPs and councils had minimal power, the Prime Minister was it. The political arraignment had a created a situation in which there was no option to appeal to the national government for Catholic leaders.

In 1969, embarrassed by demonstrations, which tended to focus on Britain's membership in the European Court of Human Rights and their denial of civil rights to some of their citizens, the British government used their bully pulpit to push the Northern Ireland government grudgingly towards change. Because they could not force the Northern Ireland Parliament to adopt the policies they wanted, all they succeeded in doing was pushing Protestant leaders currently in power far enough ahead of their constituents to lose that power. The changes were not enough to satisfy leaders of the Catholic civil rights movement who responded by calling for more protests (Callaghan 1973). The political response from Protestants in Northern Ireland to this call for change was to practice a policy of neutralization. Neutralization was the process of removing power from local elected representatives. Used first in Derry to suspend the powers of the City Council, the technique was applied throughout the rest of the territory (Rose 1976, 279). The policy effectively served to consolidate what little political power remained in the hands of the Prime Minister. Since the national government of the United Kingdom could not impose policy on Northern Ireland the lasting result of their call for reform was that by the end of 1969, the British Army was now providing security in Northern Ireland, not local police (Hadden 1996, 270).

The Prime Minister of Northern Ireland proved unwilling to provide the changes leaders of the Catholic Civil Rights movement called for. Because of systemic constraints the national government of the United Kingdom was unable to make the changes. The political system in Northern Ireland, in which the national government could not implement policy with regard to internal governance, proved unable to accommodate the Catholic Civil Rights Movement. Out of options under the current system, the leaders had to change the system itself. The Special Army Convention of 1969 saw the formation of the Provisional Irish Republican Authority whose stated goal was the destruction of the current Northern Ireland government.

The leaders of social movements are influenced by many factors. Everything from size to funding influences the strategies that they pick. The nature of the political system in which social movements operate is extremely important to the leaders who decide on strategy. Systems that have an independent judiciary, numerous electable ideologies, and a federal system encourage leaders to pick a strategy of assimilation. These characteristics make working through the existing political system the most effective way of achieving the change that social movements advocate for. Political systems that do not have these characteristics encourage leaders of social movements to pick a strategy of confrontation. The nature of the political system precludes any challenges from within. The most effective way to achieve the change that social movements advocate for is to destroy the current system.

This conclusion is true in the case of the Civil Rights Movement in the United States. The goals of the movement were realized by working through the existing system. Leaders appealed to an independent judiciary with the power of judicial review for protection of their constitutionally guaranteed rights. The court, in a series of cases from 1944 on, acted as instigator of social change with regards to the civil rights of African-Americans in the United States. After securing their rights from the court, leaders appealed to a dominant national government to protect those rights. A system in which the national government was supreme helped social movements, most notably with regard to the Little Rock Nine and the protection of black voters in the South. The passage of the Civil Rights Act of 1965, against the backdrop of continued segregation and discrimination, proved that the leaders of the Civil Rights Movement could elect politicians friendly to their cause. The system that the Civil Rights Movement in the United States operated in, one with an independent judiciary which possessed the power of judicial review, numerous electable ideologies of which black civil rights were one, and a federal system in which the national government was supreme, made the most effective strategy for leaders to pursue one of assimilation.

Additionally, because there were numerous opportunities to work through the existing political system, leaders whose groups operated outside the system faced the possibility of a crackdown. The government, with the support of the general public, takes a dim view of groups that try and destroy the political system in the United States. The arrests of such militant revolutionary groups as White Supremacists, Black Nationalists, Islamic Fascists and anarchists show this. In the United States if the leaders of Civil Rights Movement were to remain in power they had no choice but to work through to system to achieve change.

The political system that existed in Northern Ireland was a different story. The judicial branch did not have the power to review discriminatory policies of the other branches. Only Protestant candidates could get elected to Parliament; Catholicism was not an electable ideology. All political power resided with the Prime Minister of Northern Ireland and not the national government of the United Kingdom. There was no possibility that the leaders of the Catholic Civil Rights Movement in Northern Ireland could work within the system to achieve change. The existing system had to be destroyed to meet their needs.

This conclusion may seem rather straight forward, the more open a system the more likely aggrieved groups are to work through the system to seek redress. However,

70

the reason this study should matter to political scientists, is that the certain characteristics influence the strategy chosen by leaders of social movements. These are not the same as the characteristics of a liberal democracy. Additional structures, in this case the court must have the power of judicial review, minority groups must be electable somewhere in the system, and the national government must have the authority to overturn discriminatory state policy, need to also be present. Some have argued that in liberal democracies "aggrieved minorities enjoy full protection and rights of participation in the liberal state (Wilkinson 1986, 39)." As the Northern Ireland case showed, that is not always the reality. Just having a liberal democratic system does not ensure that groups with grievances will work within the system to achieve change.

The reason that the "political opportunity structure" model is more successful in predicting behavior than other models of social movements, has to do with the inclusion of the nature of the political system. "Resource mobilization theory" promotes an "overly utilitarian view of why people participate in collective action (Schrager 1985, 858)." Resources (political, material and economic) determine the strategy chosen by leaders. However, as the case studies show, the nature of the political system those resources exist in matter tremendously. I am not sure that resource mobilization theory has the tools necessary to distinguish between the different versions of democracy present in Northern Ireland and the United States. These differences proved important to the strategies chosen by leaders.

This conclusion leads to some interesting ideas about government. For the long-term stability of the state, it should be more open and present opportunities for those with grievances against the state to work through the system. If you have an independent judiciary, a federal system and numerous electable ideologies, this is more likely to happen. If this type of system is present and groups do not work through the system to address their grievances, a repression and crackdown of these groups might be viewed as legitimate by the general citizenry.

In contrast, in states with a closed political system, the government must have total control or the state will eventually fail. When groups have no option to work through the system, they will take up arms against the system. The continued existence of slavery in the world shows that this strategy of taking up arms requires the correct situation and the correct incentives for leaders to exist, including the possibility that violence can work. The government needs to be able to control the growth of movements who advocate the destruction of the state. This should be accomplished without inciting public backlash. Public support for groups that want to destroy the government can be a death sentence for the state.

The most successful states will have a political system that contains aspects of both types of system. It will have entrenched mechanisms to incorporate groups with grievances into the system. Competitive elections are an essential part of liberalized polyarchies. The general public will not tolerate violence against the system. The courts will protect minorities. Political power will be spread out amongst many different levels and many different individuals. The system will have mechanisms to make sure that governance can take place, ensuring that no one faction can hijack the political process. The most important message from this analysis is that governments, if they are to survive, must provide opportunities for individuals and groups with problems to work through the system to solve those problems. Those opportunities are not necessarily present just because a democratic system exists.

FURTHER AREAS OF STUDY

This study examined how the nature of the political system influences the strategies chosen by social movements in a qualitative manner. By necessity this was limited to examining two countries. There is the possibility of using the Freedom House Index to conduct a quantitative study of the issue. This would allow researchers to include variables that have not been included this study and see if perhaps characteristics other than an independent judiciary, a federal system and numerous electable ideologies influence leadership strategy significantly. The issue regarding the system of government in the United States is whether the system existed when the Civil Rights Movement was created was the result of conditions that existed in the Constitution or was due to changes made to the system by earlier social movements. A study of the populist/agrarian movement in the late 1800s and early 1900s in the United States would allow researchers to see if the political system was as encouraging to social movements then as it now. A study of the Civil Rights Movement in South Africa with the one in the United States would allow the comparison of two movements based on racial cleavages that pursued non-violent strategies. And finally, a study of the Maori civil rights movement in New Zealand and the "Free Quebec" movement in Canada using the criteria from above will extend the study to other democratic systems. Both of those movements remained non-violent, why?

REFERENCE

Agyeman, Opuku. 1991. "The United States Supreme Court and the Enforcement of African-American Rights: Myth and Reality." *PS: Political Science and Politics* 24: 679-684.

Anderson, Brendan. 2002. *Joe Cahill: A Life in the IRA*. Dublin: The O'Brien Press.

Axelrod, Robert. 1974. "Communications, Re: Where the Votes Come From: an Analysis of Electoral Coalitions, 1952-1968." *American Political Science Review* 68:717-720.

Barksdale, Marcellus. 1986. "Civil Rights Organization and the Indigenous Movement in Chapel Hill, N.C.. 1960-1965." *Phylon* 47:29-42.

Barritt, D.P., and C.F. Carter. 1967. *The Northern Ireland Problem*. London: Oxford University Press.

Barton, Brian and Patrick J. Roche, eds. 1994. *The Northern Ireland Question: Perspective and Policies*. Brookfield: Averbury.

Bates, Daisy. 1962. *The Long Shadow of Little Rock: A Memoir*. New York: David McKay.

BBC News. October 16, 2002. "Saddam wins 100% of vote." *BBC NEWS: World Edition*. Available at http://news.bbc.co.uk/2/hi/middle_east/2331951.stm.

Bianco, William T. and Robert H. Bates. 1990. "Cooperation by Design: Leadership, Structure, and Collective Dilemmas." *The American Political ScienceReview* 84:133-147.

Bric, Maurice J. and John Coakley, eds. *From Political Violence to Negotiated Settlement: The Winding Path to Peace in Twentieth-Century Ireland*. Dublin: University College Dublin Press.

Broussard, Albert S. 1984. "The Politics of Despair: Black San Franciscans and the Political Process, 1920-1940." *The Journal of Negro History* 69: 26-37.

Brookover, Wilbur B., Arthur Dudley and Robert L. Green. 1993. "Prince Edward County, Virginia, 30 Years After: 'A Pretty Good Place to Live." *The Journal of Negro Education* 62: 12-170.

Brysk, Alison. 1994. *The Politics of Human Rights in Argentina: Protest, Change, and Democratization*. Stanford: Stanford University Press.

Burton, Frank. 1978. *The Politics of Legitimacy: Struggles in a Belfast Community*. Boston: Routledge and Kegan Paul.

Cairns, David. 2000. "The Object of Sectarianism: The Material Reality of Sectarianism in Ulster Loyalism." *The Journal of the Royal Anthropological Institute* 6:437-452.

Callaghan, James. 1973. *A House Divided: the Dilemma of Northern Ireland*. London: Collins.

Calloway-Thomas, Carolyn and Thurmon Garner. 1996. "Daisy Bates and the Little Rock School Crisis: Forging the Way." *Journal of Black Studies* 26:616-628.

Cameron Report. 1969. *Disturbances in Northern Ireland*. Belfast: Her Majesty's Stationary Office. Available at http://cain.ulst.ac.uk/hmso/cameron.htm.

Carson, Clayborne. 1987. "Martin Luther King, Jr.: Charismatic Leadership in a Mass Struggle." *The Journal of American History* 74:448-454.

Chong, Dennis. 1991. *Collective Action and the Civil Rights Movement*. Chicago: University of Chicago Press.

Clark, Kenneth B. 1988. "The Brown Decision: Racism, Education, and Human Values." *The Journal of Negro Education* 57:125-132

Colaiaco, James A. 1986. "Martin Luther King, Jr. and the Paradox of Nonviolent Direct Action." *Phylon* 47:16-28.

Collins, William J. 2001. "Race, Roosevelt, and Wartime Production: Fair Employment in World War II Labor Markets." *The American Economic Review* 91:272-286.

Corwin, Edward S. 1950. "The Passing of Dual Federalism." *Virginia Law Review*.

Cox, Michael, Adrian Guelke and Fiona Stephen, eds. 2000. *A farewell to arms? From 'long war' to long peace in Northern Ireland*. New York: Manchester University Press.

Dahl, Robert. 1971. *Polyarchy*. New Haven: Yale University Press.

Daniels, Lee A. 1973. "The Political Career of Adam Clayton Powell." *Journal of Black Studies* 4:115-138.

Darby, John. 1997. *Scorpions in a Bottle: Conflicting Cultures in Northern Ireland*. London: Minority Rights Publication.

Decalo, Samuel. 1992. "The Process, Prospects and Constraints of Democratization of Africa." *African Affairs* 91:7-35.

Domingo, Pilar. 2000. "Judicial Independence: The Politics of the Supreme Court in Mexico." *Journal of Latin American Studies* 32:705-735.

Dua, Bhagwan D. 1983. "A Study in Executive-Judicial Conflict: The Indian Case." *Asian Survey* 23:463-483.

Duffy, Mary and Geoffrey Evans. 1996. "Building Bridges? The Political Implications of Electoral Integration for Northern Ireland." *British Journal of Political Science* 26:123-140.

Duncan, Raymond. 1976. *Latin American Politics*. New York: Praeger.

Eisenberg, Bernard. 1982. "Only for the Bourgeois? James Weldon Johnson and the NAACP, 1916-1930." *Phylon* 43: 110-124.

Eisinger, Peter K. 1973. "The Conditions of Protest Behavior in American Cities." *American Political Science Review* 67:11-28.

Elliot, Sydney and W.D. Flackes. 1999. *Conflict in Northern Ireland: An Encyclopedia*, Denver:ABC-CLIO.

Ellis, Richard. 1971. *The Jeffersonian Crisis: Courts and Politics in the Young Republic*. New York: Oxford University Press.

Fairclough, Adam. 1986. "The Preacher and the People: The Origins and Early years of the Southern Christian Leadership Conference, 1955-1959." *The Journal of Southern History* 52:403-440.

Findlay, James F. 1990. "Religion and Politics in the Sixties: The Churches and the Civil Rights Act of 1964." *The Journal of American History* 77:66-92.

Fireman, Bruce and William A. Gamson. 1979. "Utilitarian Logic in the Resource Mobilization Perspective." In *The Dynamics of Social Movements*, eds. Mayer N. Zald and J.D. McCarthy. Cambridge: Winthrop Publishers.

Fisk, Robert. 1975. *The Point of No Return: the Strike which broke the British in Ulster*. London: Times Books.

Gamer, Robert E. 1976. *The Developing Nations: A Comparative Perspective*. Boston: Allyn and Bacon.

Georges-Abeyie, Daniel E. 1983. "The Social Ecology of Bomb Threats: Dallas, Texas." *Journal of Black Studies* 13:305-320.

Goldberg, Louis C. 1968. "Ghetto Riots and Others: The Faces of Civil Disorder in 1967." *Journal of Peace Research* 5:116-132.

Goodwin, Jeff, James M. Jasper and Jaswin. 1999. "Caught in a Winding, Snarling Vine: The Structural Bias of Political Process Theory." *Sociological Forum*, 14:27-54.

Government Printing Office. 1974. *Statistical Abstract of the United States*. Washington, D.C.

Graham, Brian J. 1994. "The Search for the Common Ground: Estyn Evan's Ireland." *Transactions of the Institute of British Geographers* 19:183-201.

Groves, Harry E. 1951. "Separate but Equal — The Doctrine of Plessy v. Ferguson." *Phylon* 12:66-72.

Hadden, Tom, and Paddy Hillyard. 1973. *Justice in Northern Ireland: a Study in Social Confidence*, London: Codben Trust.

Hamilton, Charles V. 1973. *The Bench and the Ballot: Southern Federal Judges and the Black Vote*. New York: Oxford University Press.

Hamilton, Dona Copper and Charles V. Hamilton. 1992. "The Dual Agenda of African-American Organiszations since the New Deal: Social Welfare Policies and Civil Rights." *Political Science Quarterly* 107:435-452.

Heckathorn, Douglas D. 1996. "The Dynamics and Dilemmas of Collective Action." *American Sociological Review* 61: 250-277.

Hennessey, Thomas. 2001. *The Northern Ireland Peace Process: Ending the Troubles*. New York: Palgrave.

Hine, Darlene Clark. 1977. "Blacks and the Destruction of the Democratic White Primary, 1935-1944." *Journal of Negro History* 62:43-59.

Huntington, Samuel. 1968. *Political Order in Changing Societies*. New Haven: Yale University Press.

Iaryczower, Matías, Pablo T. Spiller, and Mariano Tommasi. 2002. *Judicial Independence in Unstable Environments, Argentina 1935-1998.* American Journal of Political Science 46:699-716.

Kerbo, Harold R. 1982. "Movements of Crisis and Movements of Affluence: A Critique of Deprivation and Resource Mobilization Theories." *Journal of Conflict Resolution* 26:645-663.

King Jr., Martin Luther. 2000. "I Have a Dream." *The Journal of Blacks in Higher Education* 30:121.

Kitschelt, Herbert P. 1986. "Political Opportunity Structures and Political Protest: Anti-Nuclear Movements in Four Democracies." *British Journal of Political Science* 16:57-85.

Knoke, David. 1988. "Incentives in Collective Action Organizations." *American Sociological Review* 53: 311-329.

Kollock, Peter. 1998. "Social Dilemmas: The Anatomy of Cooperation." *Annual Review of Sociology* 24:183-214.

Koopmans, Ruud. 1999. "Political. Opportunity. Structure. Some Splitting to Balance the Lumping." *Sociological Forum* 14: 93-105.

Leigh, Wilhelmina A. 1988. "The Social Preference for Fair Housing: During the Civil Rights Movement and Since." *The American Economic Review* 78:156-162.

Lewis, Earl. 1991. "More than Race Relations: A. Philip Randolph and the African-American Search for Empowerment." *Reviews in American History* 19:277-282.

Longaker, Richard P. 1956. "Andrew Jackson and the Judiciary." *Political Science Quarterly* 71:341-364.

Lyons, David. 1998. "Moral Judgment, Historical Reality and Civil Disobedience." *Philosophy and Public Affairs* 27:31-49.

Magalhães, Pedro C. 1999. "The Politics of Judicial Reform in Eastern Europe." *Comparative Politics* 32:43-62.

Marshall, T.H. 1950. *Citizenship and Social Class*. Cambridge: University Press.

McAdam, Douglas. 1983. "Tactical Innovation and the Pace of Insurgency." *American Sociological Review* 48:735-754.

McAdam, Douglas. 1992. *Political Process and the Development of Black Insurgency, 1930-1970*. Chicago: University of Chicago Press.

McAdam, Douglas. 1996. *Comparative perspectives on social movements: political opportunities, mobilizing structures, and cultural framings*. Cambridge: Cambridge University Press.

Miller, David, eds. 1998. *Rethinking Northern Ireland: Culture, Ideology and Colonialism.* London: Longman Press.

Miller, Jake C. 2000. "Harry T. Moore's Campaign for Racial Equality." *Journal of Black Studies* 31:214-231.

Moog, Robert. 1998. "Elite-Court Relations in India: An Unsatisfactory Arrangement." *Asian Survey* 38: 410-423.

Morris, Aldon D. 1999. "A Retrospective on the Civil Rights Movement: Political and Intellectual Landmarks." *Annual Review of Sociology* 25:517-539.

Narain, B.J. 1975. *Public Law in Northern Ireland.* Muckamore: Shanway Services, Inc.

National Association for the Advancement of Colored People. 2006. "Mission Statement." Available at http://www.naacp.org/about/about_mission.html.

Needler, Martin C. 1968. *Latin American Politics in Perspective.* New York: Van Nostrand.

Nelkin, Dorothy, and Susan Fallows. 1978. "The Evolution of the Nuclear Debate: The Role of Public Participation." *Annual Review of Energy* 3:275-312.

Nelson, Sarah. 1984. *Ulster's Uncertain Defenders: Protestant Political, Paramilitary, and Community Groups, and the Northern Ireland Conflict.* Syracuse: Syracuse University Press.

Nova, Fritz. 1976. "Political Innovation of the West German Federal Constitutional Court: The State of Discussion on Judicial Review." *The American Political Science Review* 70:114-125.

O'Brien, David M. 1985. "The Imperial Judiciary: Of Paper Tigers and Socio Legal Indicators." *The History Teacher* 19:33-38.

O'Neil, Terence. 1969. *Ulster at the Crossroads.* London: Faber and Faber.

Oliver, Pamela, Gerald Marwell and Ruy Teixeira. 1985. "A Theory of Critical Mass. Interdependence, Group Heterogeneity and the Production of Collective Action." *The American Journal of Sociology* 91:522-556.

Olson, Mancur. 1971. *The Logic of Collective Action.* Cambridge: Harvard University Press.

Pinard, Maurice and Jerome Kirk and Donald von Eschen. 1969. "Processes of Recruitment in the Sit-in Movement." *The Public Opinion Quarterly* 33:355-369.

Power, Paul F. 1972. "Civil Protest in Northern Ireland." *Journal of Peace Research* 9:223-236.

Reed, Harry A. 1999. "Martin Luther King, Jr.: History and Memory, Reflections on Dreams and Silences." *The Journal of Negro History* 84:150-166.

Rose, Fred. 1997. "Toward a Class-Cultural Theory of Social Movements: Reinterpreting New Social Movements." *Sociological Forum* 12:461-494.

Rose, Richard. 1971. *Governing without Consensus.* Boston: Beacon Press.

Rose, Richard. 1976. "On the Priorities of Citizenship in the Deep South and Northern Ireland." *The Journal of Politics* 38:247-291.

Rosenberg, Gerald. 1991. *The Hollow Hope: Can Courts Bring about Social Change?* Chicago: Chicago University Press.

Russo, Charles J., J. John Harris III, and Rosetta F. Sandidge. 1994. "Brown v. Board of Education at 40: A Legal History of Equal Educational Opportunities in American Public Education." *Journal of Negro Education* 63:29-309.

Scheppele, Kim Lane. 1992. "The Hollow Hope: Can Courts Bring about Social Change? A Review." *Contemporary Sociology* 24:231-233.

Schneider, Mark and Paul Teske. 1992. "Toward a Theory of the Political Entrepeneur: Evidence from Local Government." *The American Political Science Review* 86:737-747.

Schrager, Laura Schill. 1985. "Private Attitudes and Collective Action." *American Sociological Review* 50:858-859.

Schuman, Howard. 2003. "The Minority Revolution, A Review." *Contemporary Sociology* 32:434-436.

Skrentny, John David. 1998. "The Effect of the Cold War on African-American Civil Rights: American and the World Audience, 1956-1968." *Theory and Society* 27:237-285.

Smith, Calvin C. 1982. "The Politics of Evasion: Arkansas' Reaction to Smith v. Allwright, 1944." *The Journal of Negro History* 67:40-51.

Snyder, David. 1979. "Black Violence: Political Impact of the 1960s Riots. A review." *Contemporary Sociology* 8:627-628.

Steiner, Jurg. 1969. "Nonviolent Conflict Resolution in Democratic Systems: Switzerland." *The Journal of Conflict Resolution* 13:295-304.

Sterling, Dorothy. 1968. *Tear Down the Walls! A History of the American Civil Rights Movement.* Garden City: Doubleday & Company.

Tarlton, Charles D. 1965. "Symmetry and Asymmetry as Elements of Federalism: A Theoretical Speculation." *The Journal of Politics* 27:861-874.

Tarrow, Sidney. 1988. "National Politics and Collective Action: Recent Theory and Research in Western Europe and the United States." *Annual Review of Sociology* 14:421-440.

Tarrow, Sidney. 1994. *Power in Movement: Social Movements, Collective Action and Politics.* New York: Cambridge University Press.

Taylor, D. Garth. 1986. *Public Opinion and Collective Action.* Chicago: University of Chicago Press.

"The Fortieth Anniversary of the Freedom Rides." 2001. *The Journal of Black in Higher Education* 32:7.

The Washington Research Project. 1972. *The Shameful Blight: the Survival of Racial Discrimination in Voting in the South.* Washington, D.C.

Tilly, Charles. 1978. *From Mobilization to Revolution.* Reading: Addison-Wesley.

Tilly, Charles. 2004. *Social Movements, 1768-2004.* Boulder: Paradigm Publishers.

Tonge, Jonathan. 2002. *Northern Ireland: Conflict and Change.* New York: Longman.

Verner, Joel G. 1984. "The Independence of Supreme Courts in Latin America: A Review of the Literature." *Journal of Latin American Studies* 16:463-506.

Von Lazar, Arpad. 1971. *Latin American Politics: A Primer.* Boston: Allyn and Bacon.

White, Robert W. and Terry Falkenberg White. 1995. "Repression and the Liberal State: The Case of Northern Ireland, 1969-1972." *The Journal of Conflict Resolution* 39: 330-252.

Wilkinson, Paul. 1986. *Terrorism and the Liberal State.* New York: New York University Press.

Willingham, Alex. 1980. "Review: Rebellion or Revolution?" *Phylon* 41: 100-101.

Wolbrecht, Christina, Rodney E. Hero, Peri E. Arnold and Alvin B. Tillery, eds. 2005. *The Politics of Democratic Inclusion*. Philadelphia: Temple University Press.

Printed in the United States
118624LV00002B/1/P

9 783836 438568